The Smart Dentist's Guide to HIPAA and Computer Network Support
Copyright © 2018 by John A Zanazzi

ISBN 978-1-64370-551-4

The information contained in this book is not intended to serve as legal advice nor should it substitute for legal counsel. The book is not exhaustive, and readers are encouraged to seek additional detailed guidance to supplement the information contained herein. This Guide is not intended to serve as legal advice or as recommendations based on a provider or professional's specific circumstances. We encourage providers and professionals to seek expert advice when evaluating the use of this Guide. John is NOT a lawyer.

This Page left blank for notes.

About San Diego HIT:

"Our last IT guy completely messed up our database! John came in and not only fixed it but created a system where we can switch between the server and a normal computer. Awesome! You are the best IT we ever had and we have had many. John is fast and efficient. We call John with a problem and he comes immediately and resolves the issue. Upgraded all our computers and WiFi and increased their speed. Affordable, fast, efficient and to the point. Love that you don't add unnecessary items. Tells it as it is, with no techno babble."

Charlene N., San Marcos Dental Center

"John has been helping me with my computer problems for over one year and no matter what the problem is, he always able figures it out quickly and efficiently. He always arrives on time even when the call was an emergency."

Robert Sundberg, D.D.S. Dream Dental, Scottsdale, AZ

"I like John's personalized service and he is always a phone call away when we have computer problems. We recently had major server problems and John worked at the office for many days to solve the problem. John was readily available when we had any issues or questions. Since we hired John, we have encountered less computer problems because he always tries to find long term lasting solutions. Just keep doing what you're doing."

Christine, Family Dental of San Marcos, San Marcos, CA

"The talk/seminar as very interesting, did not fall asleep once. The talk had good info that we had no idea we needed to comply with. We are aware more than ever to keep patient's info private."

Heather, Rosenblatt and Firtel, San Diego, CA

"John has prompt service and comes in very quickly to phone calls. John did a proper install of a Dexis Bridge with Eagle soft on my laptop. Since we hired John we have had consistent non-problematic smooth-running computers. "

Randall Leads DDS, San Marcos, CA

"John is friendly and provides helpful information. He is knowledgeable and answers all questions. We are understanding with what we need to change in our office to become HIPAA compliant. John comes by to check in and give any help we need. The biggest benefits we have received have been helpful information and with John's flexible schedule he is able to return calls in an appropriate time frame. "

Christina Bowser, Melanie Parker Orthodontists, San Diego, CA

"I feel confident with the services provided. I just wanted to be able to work safely and not worry about HIPAA. John is experienced and thorough. "

Brock Goodman DDS Santee Orthodontists, Santee, CA

We enjoyed the great wealth of information you gave us that we can obtain HIPAA requirements and keep our patients safe and our information secure. The presentation was great and I think that you gave us a "WOW" experience. I would highly recommend this service to anyone. It was very informative. I like the second visit that gives us time to ask you questions.

Jacqui Leppke, Santee Orthodontists, Santee, CA

Table of Contents

This Page left blank for notes.

Preface

You're probably wondering why anybody would write a book about HIPAA. I have been involved in IT for over 20 years. As the past director of the Health Information Technology program at Gateway Community College, I started teaching and administrating technical areas of medical computer networks. After retiring to San Diego, I picked up where I left off and started a consulting practice specializing in the technical support of dental networks. While I was working at a client office, I was approached by an OSHA consultant. She explained to me that there was a huge need to teach the privacy aspects of HIPAA as well as the technical areas. I decided to do some research about the privacy aspects of HIPAA.

I could find a lot of information, as a matter fact I was able to find too much information. The hardest part was separating the fact from the fiction. There is an incredible amount of information available on the web. There is information that promises to get your practice to be HIPAA compliant, or HIPAA certified. (The funny thing is there is no HIPAA certification from the federal government). The best the practice can hope to achieve is to be HIPAA compliant. I thought that if I was having this much trouble deciphering HIPAA for a Dental office, there had to be a need for concise step-by-step information about HIPPA compliance written especially for Dental Offices. Although I am not an attorney and cannot give legal binding advice, I hope you can use the information in this book to stay HIPPA compliant with your practice.

Most of the best information I found was on government websites, but it was written in legalize. I used this information to write this book in what I hope will be used as a basis for your compliance program. I hope I could make it easier for you to understand.

There are many different IT vendors that say they will help your practice to move towards HIPAA compliance. Most charge a premium price tag but do not understand the Privacy and Administrative areas of HIPAA. When done correctly, compliance should not be any more expensive than managed service support. Because compliance risk actions are added before any network changes, you will have lessened risk of a privacy breach or ransomware.

Another area of miscommunication among dentists believe they are compliant or what it takes to be HIPAA compliant and stay compliant. This will help explain these common misconceptions so that you do not make these common mistakes. As a HIT HIPAA compliant consultant, I want all my clients to understand HIPAA and possible issues so that they can always understand HIPAA. This will decrease risk to the practice.

This book will help you choose the correct HIT consultant at the right price without comprising HIPAA compliance or network performance.

Remember it is possible for your network to be HIPAA compliant at a reasonable cost.

Introduction

Right now, you're probably paying for someone to maintain your computer network and you may have hired a consultant to deal with your HIPAA compliance. What if there was a way for you to complete both these tasks that and at a fraction of the cost that it would typically cost for each to be done individually.

When most dentists think of HIPAA, if they think of it at all, they tend to only think of the technical aspects of it. The truth is that most dentists believe that they already have the administration and privacy areas of HIPAA covered. They may have bought a manual, or had a risk analysis done three years ago. The fact is that neither of these solutions will prove to be adequate for HIPAA compliance. Although you may have a manual you purchased from the society, which is compressive, this manual must be personalized, updated and followed.

If they are relying on their "IT Guy" without vetting him, they may be setting themselves up for a violation or a data breach. A Risk analysis must be redone at a minimum of every year. Because the risk analysis has many technical questions, typically a Dentist will just pass this task to their "IT Guy" believing the "IT Guy" has HIPAA under control. According to HIPAA, not only does your "IT Guy" have to understand HIPAA, he is a Business Associate. Because most requests to access ePHI involve the computer network, he should help regulate your other Business Associates. Because Business Associates often will have access to your ePHI, it is imperative that you analyze each request for network access.

When it comes to the technical part of HIPAA, if a person you choose to safeguard your computer network (in addition to your practice's privacy policy) does not understand HIPAA, you run the risk of not being ready for a HIPAA audit. If you are relying on their "IT Guy" without screening him, you may be setting yourselves up for a HIPAA violation or a data breach. Most IT guys do not know HIPAA

Risk analyses must be redone at a minimum of every year. More often when there are major network changes.

Whenever I talk to dentists about the technical aspects of HIPAA, their eyes become glassed over and I could tell there are 1 million other places they'd rather be at that point. So, they go out and find an IT guy who says that he can handle the technical aspects of the network, but is he handling them in a way that will contribute to HIPAA compliance?

Some typical technical aspects of HIPAA include computer security protections. This is so that there is no theft of your patient information. Although most "IT guys" know to install antivirus on your computers, they do not document and monitor it. If you do not continually monitor and maintain computers on your network, you run into the risk of losing the compliance that you worked so hard to achieve.

The truth is that when IT guys work on your computer network, they may be doing best practices with respect to computer security. But when it comes to HIPAA compliance they stop short. For a network to be considered HIPAA compliant, there are other things that must be done, such as documentation and keeping track of ePHI. You must document the location of where the ePHI is, both at rest and in motion. They must send monthly security notices. Did you know that anyone who encounters your ePHI must have a Business associate agreement? This includes lawyers, accountants, IT contractors, billing companies, cloud storage services, email encryption services, web hosts and printer companies. You do have a BAA with each of these venders, don't you?

If HIPAA was only technical and you chose a HIPAA compliant MSP, (explained later) you could sleep easy knowing your network is safe and secure from data breaches, HIPAA audits and ransomware. But according to the ONC, most HIPAA violations in smaller dental practices are the privacy kind, not technical kind. These are caused by not a computer hacker but by a staff member not following your practice policies and procedures. (You do have them right) These are usually caused by somebody in your office disclosing private information. The cause of this is usually caused by lack of yearly mandatory HIPAA training. The policies and procedures not only have to be written with the practice in mind. Everyone including you "IT Guy" must follow them. Another area that most practices miss is the practice disaster recovery plan. I hope you use this book to find the best fit for you practice by using the checklists, forms and questions. These will help you find the best person for your IT needs.

This Page left blank for notes.

Chapter One
If you don't worry about HIPAA, it will not go away

Right now, thinking about HIPAA is probably the last thing on your mind. In addition to being a full-time dentist, you have a business to run. Along with running your business comes the task getting out bills, managing your staff, and making sure that your office is running efficiently. Getting someone to cover for the front office person who called in sick right now is your most pressing issue, not HIPAA.

Unless you've been living in a cave the past year, it's almost impossible to watch the news or read the newspaper without hearing about different medical facilities being hacked. You try to make yourself feel better by saying there had to be an extremely talented hacker from a foreign country that hacked these practice networks and caused their patient data to be spread throughout the dark web. You think, shoot these companies that have a much higher IT budget than I do, and they got hacked so there is nothing you can do to stop it. Or you think you're too small, they would never take time to try to hack you. Plus, your current patient list isn't that big. The scary thought is that if you get hacked, you must worry about not only your current patients but all your past patients. Even though a patient may not be an active patient, their ePHI is still in your Electronic Dental Record.

If you thought things couldn't get worse, the Federal Trade Commission is also getting into the compliance "game". You need to do more than just meet the requirements for a HIPAA-compliant practice. Your business must consider all your statements to consumers to make sure that, taken together, they don't create a deceptive or misleading statement. Even if you believe your practice meets all the rules required by the HIPAA Privacy Rule, if the information surrounding the authorization is deceptive or misleading, that's a violation of the FTC Act. According to the FTC, a HIPAA breach is not only a HIPAA Violation it may be eligible for a fine by the FTC.

According to a recent study over 40% of patients will switch medical providers if a breach occurs, and the chances of a breach occurring are much higher than you having to undergo a federal audit. Unfortunately, all it takes is a wrong click, and your patient data is on the dark web. Now you may be saying to yourself that all my data is inside of my patient record system, and that is defended against hackers by a password. The problem is that one bad click, one Facebook message, or even going to the wrong website, can allow a bad guy to put malware on your system which can capture the keystrokes to get inside your EHR. I also know you're saying to yourself that your staff is not gullible enough to click on those links. Plus, you think because all your staff members are young people and young people understand computers so much better than you it could never happen. But this is the way most patient data gets on to dark web.

Did you know that if one to 499 medical records are breached you must notify the ONC and because you are in California, the California State Attorney general within 60 days? In addition, if there are more than 500 records you must notify the media. You also must notify each one of your patients. How would you like to send a letter starting, Dearest Patient, because of lax security on my part your medical record is now found in the dark web?

I don't like to be a fear monger, but the chances of this happening are real. I wrote this book because although there is so much HIPAA information out there, there is even more miscommunication, I hope you use this book to not only understand HIPAA, but to use it help stop the proliferation of data breaches. These affects everyone in the world. I want to show a how a little preparation now will go a long way to stop these data breaches.

Chapter Two
Inaccurate Ways Dentists believe they are complying with HIPAA

- **We don't need it because we don't take any insurance:**
  Taking or not taking insurance is not a prerequisite for HIPAA.
- **We don't have any electronic records on our computers, we are all paper:** Two of the three areas of HIPAA; Privacy and Policies and procedures deal areas of your practice that are not electronic. HIPAA deals with paper records and verbal discussion of a patient record. It is not totally dependent on electronic records, just patient records.
- **We have a compliant EHR and the vendor takes care of it.**
  Your EHR is just one part of your practice that is governed by HIPAA. Your data must get from your workstation or tablet into the server. Plus are you sure your Practice Management System is complaint?
- **We store all our data in the cloud; therefore, our cloud provider takes care of all security**. That is all well and good but just because your cloud says they are safe guarding your data does not mean that they are. Think of Equifax, Yahoo, AOL and the list keeps going and going.
- **I'm rolling the dice, they won't catch me because my practice is too small.** So, you decide to do nothing and just roll the dice and pay any fines if you get audited. I mean the risk of being audited is a low rate. In the past, the odds of getting audited were less than hitting lotto for $1 billion dollars. And you know you're not going to hit the lottery anytime soon so you are safe, right. But getting audited by the federal government and having to pay a fine could be the least of your worries. In California along with HIPAA, we also have the CMIA, or Confidentiality of Medical Information Act (CMIA). What about ransomware?
- **Dentists don't have to comply with HIPAA:** HIPAA applies to covered entities of all shapes and sizes. If you store, process, transmit, maintain, or touch protected health information (PHI) in any way, you must be compliant.

- **It's too much work and it will never pay off:** Did you know, according to Cintas, 40% of patients would change doctors/dentists if their network was breached? Can you afford to lose 40% of your patients?

- **Nobody wants my data they are more interested in big companies**: in an article by Charles Ornstein, "it's often little-noticed smaller-scale violations of medical privacy — the ones that affect only one or two people — that inflict the most harm. Driven by personal animus, jealousy or a desire for retribution, small breaches involving sensitive health details is spurring disputes and legal battles across the country."

- **It's too expensive to be compliant:** In addition to having to pay possible audit fines, if your practice gets ransomware you may have to pay these crooks money to get your data back and file a breach report with the state and HHS. This year, the Ponemon Institute calculated the average healthcare data breach costs $380 per record. The average global cost per record for all industries is now $141, with healthcare data breach costs more than 2.5 times the global average. Last year, average healthcare data breach costs were $402 per record. The average cost of a breach in the United States across all industries is $225 per record, up from $221 in 2016. This includes both you active and inactive patients.

- **We don't have ePHI:** But you do have protected health information (PHI) includes a patient's name, their Social Security Number, address, birthday, or a dozen other data points. So, if you store, process, transmit, maintain, or touch PHI in any way, you must be compliant.

- **All the addressable safeguards do not apply to me. I will just ignore them.** Addressable does not mean optional, either you must complete the requirement or explain in detail why you did not do them and substituted another safeguard. It is often easier just to follow the original safeguard.

Chapter Three

How does HIPAA apply to me and common HIPAA misconceptions?

But right now, you don't even know if HIPAA applies to your practice. Or you still think you are HIPAA compliant.

Here are some of the inaccurate ways that Dentists think their practice is **HIPAA compliant:**

My practice is already HIPAA compliant so I don't need to worry about it: A practice may consider itself compliant, but remember that HIPAA requirements are commonly amended, so practices need to make sure they're continually up to date by doing annual risk-assessments, which can include network diagnostics, penetration testing, and even backup verification and testing.

They'll also need a compliance officer responsible for making sure policies and procedures are up to date (we'll get to compliance officers later).

Also, don't forget that HIPAA compliance affects a practice and anyone it works with. "One Guy's Opinion," Guy Baroan says HIPAA pretty much trickles down to everyone. If a practice's vendors (including managed service providers) haven't signed business associate agreements, that practice isn't compliant. And according to an article by McDermott, Will, and Emory, phase two of the Office for Civil Rights' audits will include audits of business associates. This means practices want to have business associate agreements with their partners.

I purchased a Manual from a Society or I downloaded and changed a template I found online: These must be customized for your practice. You also must follow the policies and procedures. If you are audited, you must demonstrate that you are following the policies and procedures manual.

We filled out a checklist or we bought software from … So, we are okay. Once again these must be designed for your practice. You also must follow the policies and procedures. Someone also must fill out the check list or answer the software questions.

We signed a business associate agreement, BAA, with my vendors therefore they take all the risk: Don't forget that HIPAA compliance affects a practice and anyone it works with. In an interview about HIPAA compliance and MSPs, McDermott states, HIPAA pretty much trickles down to everyone. If a practice's vendors (including managed service providers) haven't signed business associate agreements, that practice isn't compliant. And per an article by McDermott, Will, and Emory, phase two of the Office for Civil Rights' audits will include audits of business associates. This means practices want to have business associate agreements with their partners.

We are using encrypted email so we are okay: Only one part of HIPAA deals with encrypted email. (If a bad guy has your email password, he can unencrypt your emails)

My IT guy has it covered: Does your IT guy know about privacy and sanction policies? The IT aspect of HIPAA is only half of the story. Once everything is on the network, nurses, Dentists, and any employees in the practice need to understand how to keep data secure and safe. They need to know what HIPAA is and what they need to do to comply. This typically involves new processes they may not want to learn. Many times, even once all safeguards are in place, it can be difficult to get doctors to perform the necessary processes that keep them in compliance. In any case, practices need to understand that training and education on HIPAA privacy is every bit as important as the technology aspect of HIPAA.

I have a Privacy officer: Does your privacy officer continually monitor the HHS, ONC for changes in the HIPAA and the state of California for change in the CMIA laws. Do they spend hours monitoring the latest computer and internet threats? At the very least is it documented?

My office manager did it: Does your office manager understand computer viruses, firewalls, backup and recovery?

I have a manual that was done a couple years ago: All employees, volunteers, trainees and others who work under the control of the covered entity must be trained on the policies and procedures developed to comply with HIPAA. All new employees must be trained within a reasonable time after they join the workforce and additional training must occur within a reasonable time after any material change in a policy or procedure. All training activity must be documented and kept for six years. Covered entities must review and modify their security measures to continue protecting e-PHI in a changing environment. The manual must be updated as situations change.

§ 164.316(b) (2)(iii) The Updates implementation specification requires covered entities to: "Review documentation periodically, and update as needed, in response to environmental or operational changes affecting the security of the electronic protected health information." The need for review and update will vary based on a covered entity's documentation review frequency and/or the volume of environmental or operational changes that affect the security of EPHI. This implementation specification requires covered entities to manage their documentation so that it reflects the current status of their security plans and procedures implemented to comply with the Security Rule.

My practice is already HIPAA compliant so I don't need to worry: A practice may consider itself compliant, but remember that HIPAA requirements are commonly amended, so practices need to make sure they're continually up to date by doing annual risk-assessments, which can include network diagnostics, penetration testing, and even backup verification and testing. HIPAA compliance is a continuous process.

I don't want to hire a compliance officer: Per the U.S. Department of Health and Human Services, HIPAA is designed to keep both small and large practices in compliance. Some smaller practices may not be able to hire a person specifically for compliance, but practices do need to designate someone as a privacy official or compliance officer. This is somebody who is responsible for developing and implementing privacy policies and procedures. A privacy official can be somebody the practice already employs, but this position does require special knowledge.

Our Dental Software is HIPAA certified: This brings me to another typical misinformation perpetrated by the Practice Management system companies. This is that because you are using their program, you are HIPAA compliant. Their reasoning behind this is that because you need a username and password to access the database of ePHI the software is secure. But you must monitor who is accessing the software. Also, the software must stay compliant by applying software and security patches, the problem is that if the computer network is breached this could lead to a data breach from malware being installed on a workstation.

All our data is in the cloud: Another miscommunication between doctors and vendors is that if their software is in the cloud then the cloud vendor is responsible for the HIPAA compliance. This is just not true, although you may have offloaded the task of hosting your network, you still are responsible to monitor your software. And sometimes these vendors are just guilty of bad security practices. You are also responsible for backing up your data.

Chapter Four
The 10 Most common HIPAA violations and preventative measures to help keep your practice in compliance

1. **Employees disclosing private information:** It is important to have training in place so that staff will not give out information they are not authorized to give out.
2. **Medical records mishandling**: Staff must be careful so that patient charts and information is not in plain sight. The office must also make sure that computer screens are not able to be seen by anyone other than the intended person who using the computer.
3. **Lost or Stolen Devices**: Many doctors believe because their data is in the cloud they don't have to worry about ePHI on laptops and mobile devices. PHI often can be found in other areas of the computers such as my documents, emails and possibly downloads. A good way to safeguard this is to encrypt all data on the drive.
4. **Texting patient information**: Texting has become a useful way to communicate quickly. But you should be careful not to disclose private information in the text. There are programs available that will allow secure texting.
5. **Social Media**: Although people often post many different things online unless the doctor has specific permission to post on social media, this is a violation. Although many people don't think of photographs as PHI, posting pictures without a patient release is a HIPAA violation.
6. **Employees illegally accessing patient files**: Unless you have a specific reason to access a patient record, you have no legal right to see the any private information. Proper training will help lessen this risk.
7. **Social breaches**: A social breach is when a staff member casually mentions that somebody was in the office. Typically,

will typically this occurs in smaller communities there is a higher probability that someone will know everyone else.

8. **Authorization Requirements:** For the most part, the only time it is okay to release information without patient consent is when it is for the treatment of the patient or payment of treatment. The sale or use of private information is strictly prohibited unless the patient authorizes its use for this purpose.

9. **Accessing patient information on home computers**: With the added convenience of being able to access patient records at home comes to risk of somebody seeing information they should not see. When accessing patient information at home or somewhere other than the office HIPAA rules still apply.

10. **Lack of training**: Everyone in the office who comes into contact ePHI must have a training at a minimum every year on HIPAA policy. In addition, the staff must be reminded periodically about patient record safety.

Chapter Five

Latest OCR Enforcement Results as of Sept. 30, 2017

Since the compliance date of the Privacy Rule in April 2003, OCR has received over 163,277 HIPAA complaints and has initiated over 847compliance reviews. They have resolved ninety-eight percent of the complaint cases (159,633).

OCR has investigated and resolved over 25,373 cases by requiring changes in privacy practices and corrective actions by, or providing technical assistance to, HIPAA covered entities and their business associates. Corrective actions obtained by OCR from these entities have resulted in change that is systemic and that affects all the individuals they serve. OCR has successfully enforced the HIPAA Rules by applying corrective measures in all cases where an investigation indicates noncompliance by the covered entity or their business associate, which may include settling with the entity in lieu of imposing a civil money penalty. To date, OCR has settled 52 such cases resulting in a total dollar amount of $72,929,182.00. OCR has investigated complaints against many different types of entities including: national pharmacy chains, major medical centers, group health plans, hospital chains, and small provider offices. In another 11,317 cases, our investigations found no violation had occurred. Additionally, in 22,902 cases, OCR has intervened early and provided technical assistance to HIPAA covered entities, their business associates, and individuals exercising their rights under the Privacy Rule, without the need for an investigation.

In the rest of our completed cases, (100,041) OCR determined that the complaint did not present an eligible case for enforcement. These include cases in which:

- OCR lacks jurisdiction under HIPAA. For example, in cases alleging a violation by an entity not covered by HIPAA;

- The complaint is untimely, or withdrawn by the filer. The activity described does not violate the HIPAA Rules;
- The activity described does not violate the HIPAA Rules. For example, in cases where the covered entity has disclosed protected health information in circumstances in which the Privacy Rule permits such a disclosure.
- From the compliance date to the present, the compliance issues investigated most are, compiled cumulatively, in order of frequency:
- Impermissible uses and disclosures of protected health information;
- Lack of safeguards of protected health information;
- Lack of patient access to their protected health information;
- Use or disclosure of more than the minimum necessary protected health information; and
- Lack of administrative safeguards of electronic protected health information.

The most common types of covered entities that have been required to take corrective action to achieve voluntary compliance are, in order of frequency:

- Private Practices;
- General Hospitals;
- Outpatient Facilities;
- Pharmacies; and
- Health Plans (group health plans and health insurance issuers).

Referrals: OCR refers to the Department of Justice (DOJ) for criminal investigation appropriate cases involving the knowing disclosure or obtaining of protected health information in violation of the Rules. As of the date of this summary, OCR made 638 such referrals to DOJ.

https://www.hhs.gov/hipaa/for-professionals/compliance-enforcement/data/enforcement-highlights/index.html

Chapter Six
HIPAA Explained

So, you go online and do a search for HIPAA. And you find that there are many different products, many different systems and many different consultants. Some claim to "Make you HIPAA certified". Still you don't know what it means to be HIPAA certified. So, then you go to the ONC site and read up about HIPAA. (BTW there is no federal HIPAA certification, the best you can be is HIPAA compliant) And the more you read, the more confused you become. You are an intelligent person, you became a dentist, but you have no idea what these rules and regulations mean. I mean you got into dentistry to practice dentistry, not to become a lawyer or a computer tech.

That brings up another point what exactly is does it mean to be HIPAA compliant. As a dentist, you know that you are subject to HIPAA laws. But with the constant never-ending tasks of being a dentist and running your practice, HIPAA just seems to be pushed to the back the back of your mind. You know you must do something because it is required by both state and federal laws. You just don't know where to begin. At the very least you don't even know what it means to be compliant or more importantly how to stay compliant.

You not even sure that you understand what is HIPAA compliance and what does it take to stay in compliance. According to the Office for Civil Rights Headquarters webpage:

"The Health Insurance Portability and Accountability Act of 1996 (HIPAA) required the Secretary of the U.S. Department of Health and Human Services (HHS) to develop regulations protecting the privacy and security of certain health information.

To fulfill this requirement, HHS published what are commonly known as the HIPAA Privacy Rule and the HIPAA Security Rule. The Privacy Rule, or Standards for Privacy of Individually Identifiable Health Information, establishes national standards for the protection of certain health information. The Security Standards for the Protection of Electronic Protected Health Information (the Security Rule) establish a national set of security standards for protecting certain health information that is held or transferred in electronic form. The Security Rule operationalizes the protections contained in the Privacy Rule by addressing the technical and non-technical safeguards that organizations called "covered entities" must put in place to secure individuals' "electronic protected health information" (e-PHI). Within HHS, the Office for Civil Rights (OCR) has responsibility for enforcing the Privacy and Security Rules with voluntary compliance activities and civil money penalties."

The HIPAA privacy rule establishes national standards to protect individual's medical records and other personal health information and applies to health plans health care clearinghouse is and those healthcare providers that conduct certain healthcare transactions of electronically. The rule requires appropriate safeguards to protect the privacy of personal health information, and sets limits and conditions on the uses and authorizations that may be made of such information without patient authorization the will also give patient rights over their health information, including rights to examine and obtain a copy of the health records and request corrections.

This is a summary of key elements of the Security Rule and not a complete or comprehensive guide to compliance.

The Security Rule requires covered entities to maintain reasonable and appropriate administrative, technical, and physical safeguards for protecting e-PHI.

Specifically, covered entities must:

1. Ensure the confidentiality, integrity, and availability of all e-PHI they create, receive, maintain or transmit;
2. Identify and protect against reasonably anticipated threats to the security or integrity of the information;
3. Protect against reasonably anticipated, impermissible uses or disclosures; and
4. Ensure compliance by their workforce.

The Security Rule defines "confidentiality" to mean that e-PHI is not available or disclosed to unauthorized persons. The Security Rule's confidentiality requirements support the Privacy Rule's prohibitions against improper uses and disclosures of PHI. The Security rule also promotes the two additional goals of maintaining the integrity and availability of e-PHI. Under the Security Rule, "integrity" means that e-PHI is not altered or destroyed in an unauthorized manner. "Availability" means that e-PHI is accessible and usable on demand by an authorized person.

HHS recognizes that covered entities range from the smallest provider to the largest, multi-state health plan. Therefore, the Security Rule is flexible and scalable to allow covered entities to analyze their own needs and implement solutions appropriate for their specific environments. What is appropriate for a covered entity will depend on the nature of the covered entity's business, as well as the covered entity's size and resources.

Therefore, when a covered entity is deciding which security measures to use, the Rule does not dictate those measures but requires the covered entity to consider:

- Its size, complexity, and capabilities,
- Its technical, hardware, and software infrastructure,
- The costs of security measures, and
- The likelihood and possible impact of potential risks to e-PHI.

Covered entities must review and modify their security measures to continue protecting e-PHI in a changing environment.

Risk Analysis and Management

- The Administrative Safeguards provisions in the Security Rule require covered entities to perform risk analysis as part of their security management processes.

The risk analysis and management provisions of the Security Rule are addressed separately here because, by helping to determine which security measures are reasonable and appropriate for a covered entity, risk analysis affects the implementation of all the safeguards contained in the Security Rule.

- A risk analysis process includes, but is not limited to, the following activities:
  - o Evaluate the likelihood and impact of potential risks to e-PHI;
  - o Implement appropriate security measures to address the risks identified in the risk analysis;
  - o Document the chosen security measures and, where required, the rationale for adopting those measures; and
  - o Maintain continuous, reasonable, and appropriate security protections.

Risk analysis should be an ongoing process, in which a covered entity regularly reviews its records to track access to e-PHI and detect security incidents, periodically evaluates the effectiveness of security measures put in place, and regularly reevaluates potential risks to e-PHI.

Administrative Safeguards

- **Security Management Process.** As explained in the previous section, a covered entity must identify and analyze potential risks to e-PHI, and it must implement security measures that reduce risks and vulnerabilities to a reasonable and appropriate level.
- **Security Personnel.** A covered entity must designate a security official who is responsible for developing and implementing its security policies and procedures.
- **Information Access Management.** Consistent with the Privacy Rule standard limiting uses and disclosures of PHI to the "minimum necessary," the Security Rule requires a covered entity to implement policies and procedures for authorizing access to e-PHI only when

such access is appropriate based on the user or recipient's role (role-based access).

- **Workforce Training and Management.** A covered entity must provide for appropriate authorization and supervision of workforce members who work with e-PHI. A covered entity must train all workforce members regarding its security policies and procedures, and must have and apply appropriate sanctions against workforce members who violate its policies and procedures.
- **Evaluation**. A covered entity must perform a periodic assessment of how well its security policies and procedures meet the requirements of the Security Rule.

Physical Safeguards

- **Facility Access and Control.** A covered entity must limit physical access to its facilities while ensuring that authorized access is allowed.
- **Workstation and Device Security.** A covered entity must implement policies and procedures to specify proper use of and access to workstations and electronic media. A covered entity also must have in place policies and procedures regarding the transfer, removal, disposal, and re-use of electronic media, to ensure appropriate protection of electronic protected health information (e-PHI).

Technical Safeguards

- **Access Control.** A covered entity must implement technical policies and procedures that allow only authorized persons to access electronic protected health information (e-PHI).
- **Audit Controls.** A covered entity must implement hardware, software, and/or procedural mechanisms to record and examine access and other activity in information systems that contain or use e-PHI.
- **Integrity Controls.** A covered entity must implement policies and procedures to ensure that e-PHI is not improperly altered or destroyed. Electronic measures must be put in place to confirm that e-PHI has not been improperly altered or destroyed.

- **Transmission Security.** A covered entity must implement technical security measures that guard against unauthorized access to e-PHI that is being transmitted over an electronic network.

Required and Addressable Implementation Specifications

- Covered entities are required to comply with every Security Rule "Standard." However, the Security Rule categorizes certain implementation specifications within those standards as "addressable," while others are "required." The "required" implementation specifications must be implemented. **The "addressable" designation does not mean that an implementation specification is optional.** However, it permits covered entities to determine whether the addressable implementation specification is reasonable and appropriate for that covered entity. If it is not, the Security Rule allows the covered entity to adopt an alternative measure that achieves the purpose of the standard, if the alternative measure is reasonable and appropriate.

Organizational Requirements

- **Covered Entity Responsibilities.** <u>If a covered entity knows of an activity or practice of the business associate that constitutes a material breach or violation of the business associate's obligation, the covered entity must take reasonable steps to cure the breach or end the violation.</u> Violations include the failure to implement safeguards that reasonably and appropriately protect e-PHI.
- **Business Associate Contracts.** HHS developed regulations relating to business associate obligations and business associate contracts under the HITECH Act of 2009.

Policies and Procedures and Documentation Requirements

- A covered entity must adopt reasonable and appropriate policies and procedures to comply with the provisions of the Security Rule. A covered entity must maintain, until six years after the later of the date of their creation or last effective date, written security policies and procedures and written records of required actions, activities or assessments.

- **Updates.** A covered entity must periodically review and update its documentation in response to environmental or organizational changes that affect the security of electronic protected health information (e-PHI).

State Law

- **Preemption.** In general, State laws that are contrary to the HIPAA regulations are preempted by the federal requirements, which means that the federal requirements will apply. "Contrary" means that it would be impossible for a covered entity to comply with both the State and federal requirements, or that the provision of State law is an obstacle to accomplishing the full purposes and objectives of the Administrative Simplification provisions of HIPAA.

Enforcement and Penalties for Noncompliance

- **Compliance.** The Security Rule establishes a set of national standards for confidentiality, integrity and availability of e-PHI. The Department of Health and Human Services (HHS), Office for Civil Rights (OCR) is responsible for administering and enforcing these standards, in concert with its enforcement of the Privacy Rule, and may conduct complaint investigations and compliance reviews.
- Learn more about enforcement and penalties in the Privacy Rule Summary - PDF - PDF and on OCR's Enforcement Rule page.

Compliance Dates

- **Compliance Schedule.** All covered entities, except "small health plans," must have been compliant with the Security Rule by April 20, 2005. Small health plans had until April 20, 2006 to comply.

Copies of the Rule and Related Materials

- See our Combined Regulation Text of All Rules section of our site for the full suite of HIPAA Administrative Simplification Regulations and HIPAA for Professionals for additional guidance material.

The FTC is also getting involved. Once you've drafted a HIPAA authorization, you can't forget the FTC Act. The FTC Act prohibits companies from engaging in deceptive or unfair acts or practices in or affecting commerce. Among other things, this means that companies must not mislead consumers about what is happening with their health information.

(https://www.ftc.gov/tips-advice/business-center/guidance/sharing-consumer-health-information-look-hipaa-ftc-act)

Chapter Seven

"The Confidentiality of Medical Information Act (CMIA)"

And if that isn't enough a couple years ago many states, California included, now have the power to not only in act fines but in the cases of extreme law-breaking, award jail sentences. So now in addition to possibly being fined by the federal government you also must worry about a jail term by an overzealous state attorney general. So along with HIPAA in California you must obey:

"The Confidentiality of Medical Information Act (CMIA)"

The Confidentiality of Medical Information Act (CMIA) is a state law that adds to the federal protection of personal medical records under the Health Information Portability and Accountability Act (HIPAA). CMIA protects the confidentiality of individually identifiable medical information obtained by a health care provider and includes the following:

- CMIA prohibits a health care provider, health care service plan, or contractor from disclosing medical information regarding a patient, enrollee, or subscriber without first obtaining an authorization, except as specified. CMIA requires a health care provider, health care service plan, pharmaceutical company, or contractor who creates, maintains, preserves, stores, abandons, destroys, or disposes of medical records to do so in a manner that preserves the confidentiality of the information contained within those records.
- CMIA defines "medical information" to mean any individually identifiable information, in electronic or physical form, in possession of or derived from a provider of health care, health care service plan, pharmaceutical company, or contractor regarding a patient's medical history, mental or physical condition, or treatment. "Individually identifiable" means that the

medical information includes or contains any element of personal identifying information sufficient to allow identification of the individual, such as the patient's name, address, electronic mail address, telephone number, or social security number, or other information that reveals the individual's identity.

- Any individual may bring an action against any person or entity that has negligently released confidential information or records, for either or both nominal damages of $1,000 and the amount of actual damages, if any, sustained by the patient. It shall not be necessary to prove that the plaintiff suffered or was threatened with actual damages to recovery nominal damages.

Taken From: https://consumercal.org/about-cfc/cfc-education-foundation/cfceducation-foundationyour-medical-privacy-rights/confidentiality-of-medical-information-act/

Any person or entity who knowingly and willfully obtains, discloses, or uses medical information in violation of CMIA shall be liable for an administrative fine not to exceed $2,500 per violation.* * https://leginfo.ca.gov/pub/11-12/bill/asm/ab_0401-0450/ab_439_bill_20120922_chaptered.html

Chapter Eight

The Top 10 Myths of a Security Risk Analysis taken from www.healthit.gov.

As with any new program or regulation, there may be misinformation making the rounds.

The following is a top 10 list distinguishing fact from fiction about a Security Risk Analysis.

1. The security risk analysis is optional for small providers.

False. All providers who are "covered entities" under HIPAA are required to perform a risk analysis. In addition, all providers who want to receive EHR incentive payments must conduct a risk analysis.

2. Simply installing a certified EHR fulfills the security risk analysis MU requirement.

False. Even with a certified EHR, you must perform a full security risk analysis. Security requirements address all electronic protected health information you maintain, not just what is in your EHR.

3. My EHR vendor took care of everything I need to do about privacy and security.

False. Your EHR vendor may be able to provide information, assistance, and training on the privacy and security aspects of the EHR product. However, EHR vendors are not responsible for making their products compliant with HIPAA Privacy and Security Rules. It is solely your responsibility to have a complete risk analysis conducted.

4. I must outsource the security risk analysis.

False. It is possible for small practices to do risk analysis themselves using self-help tools. However, doing a thorough and professional risk analysis that will stand up to a compliance review will require expert knowledge that could be obtained through services of an experienced outside professional.

5. A checklist will suffice for the risk analysis requirement.

False. Checklists can be useful tools, especially when starting a risk analysis, but they fall short of performing a systematic security risk analysis or documenting that one has been performed.

6.   There is a specific risk analysis method that I must follow.

False. A risk analysis can be performed in countless ways. OCR has issued Guidance on Risk Analysis Requirements of the Security Rule. This guidance assists organizations in identifying and implementing the most effective and appropriate safeguards to secure e-PHI.

7.   My security risk analysis only needs to look at my EHR.

False. Review all electronic devices that store, capture, or modify electronic protected health information. Include your EHR hardware and software and devices that can access your EHR data (e.g., your tablet computer, your practice manager's mobile phone). Remember that copiers also store data. Please see U.S. Department of Health and Human Services (HHS) guidance on remote use.

8.   I only need to do a risk analysis once.

False. To comply with HIPAA, you must continue to review, correct or modify, and

9.   Before I attest for an EHR incentive program, I must fully mitigate all risks.

False. The EHR incentive program requires correcting any deficiencies (identified during the risk analysis) during the reporting period, as part of its risk management process.

10. Each year, I'll have to completely redo my security risk analysis.

False. Perform the full security risk analysis as you adopt an EHR. Each year or when changes to your practice or electronic systems occur, review and update the prior analysis for changes in risks. Under the Meaningful Use Programs, reviews are required for each EHR reporting period. For EPs, the EHR reporting period will be 90 days or a full calendar year, depending on the EP's year of participation in the program.

A risk analysis should be used as a starting point to see what needs to be addressed.

Chapter Nine
Introduction to a Proper Risk Analysis

The Office for Civil Rights (OCR) is responsible for issuing annual guidance on the provisions in the HIPAA Security Rule. (45 C.F.R. §§ 164.302 – 318.) This series of guidance will assist organizations in identifying and implementing the most effective and appropriate administrative, physical, and technical safeguards to secure electronic protected health information (e- PHI). The guidance materials will be developed with input from stakeholders and the public, and will be updated as appropriate.

We begin the series with the risk analysis requirement in § 164.308(a) (1) (ii) (A). Conducting a risk analysis is the first step in identifying and implementing safeguards that comply with and carry out the standards and implementation specifications in the Security Rule. Therefore, a risk analysis is foundational, and must be understood in detail before OCR can issue meaningful guidance that specifically addresses safeguards and technologies that will best protect electronic health information.

The guidance is not intended to provide a one-size-fits-all blueprint for compliance with the risk analysis requirement. Rather, it clarifies the expectations of the Department for organizations working to meet these requirements. An organization should determine the most appropriate way to achieve compliance, considering the characteristics of the organization and its environment.

We note that some of the content contained in this guidance is based on recommendations of the National Institute of Standards and Technology (NIST). NIST, a federal agency, publishes freely available material in the public domain, including guidelines. Although only federal agencies are required to follow guidelines set by NIST, the guidelines represent the industry standard for good business practices with respect to standards for securing e-PHI. Therefore, non-federal organizations may find their content valuable when developing and performing compliance activities.

All e-PHI created, received, maintained or transmitted by an organization is subject to the Security Rule. The Security Rule requires entities to evaluate risks and vulnerabilities in their environments and to implement reasonable and appropriate security measures to protect against reasonably anticipated threats or hazards to the security or integrity of e-PHI. Risk analysis is the first step in that process.

We understand that the Security Rule does not prescribe a specific risk analysis methodology, recognizing that methods will vary dependent on the size, complexity, and capabilities of the organization. Instead, the Rule identifies risk analysis as the foundational element in the process of achieving compliance, and it establishes several objectives that any methodology adopted must achieve.

Risk Analysis Requirements under the Security Rule

The Security Management Process standard in the Security Rule requires organizations to

"[i]implement policies and procedures to prevent, detect, contain, and correct security violations." (45 C.F.R. § 164.308(a)(1).) Risk analysis is one of four required implementation specifications that provide instructions to implement the Security Management Process standard. Section 164.308(a)(1)(ii)(A) states:

RISK ANALYSIS (Required).

Conduct an accurate and thorough assessment of the potential risks and vulnerabilities to the confidentiality, integrity, and availability of electronic protected health information held by the [organization].

The following questions adapted from NIST Special Publication (SP) 800-66 are examples organizations could consider as part of a risk analysis. These sample questions are not prescriptive and merely identify issues an organization may wish to consider in implementing the Security Rule:

- Have you identified the e-PHI within your organization? This includes e-PHI that you create, receive, maintain or transmit.

- What are the external sources of e-PHI? For example, do vendors or consultants create, receive, maintain or transmit e-PHI?

- What are the human, natural, and environmental threats

40

to information systems that contain e-PHI?

In addition to an express requirement to conduct a risk analysis, the Rule indicates that risk analysis is a necessary tool in reaching substantial compliance with many other standards and implementation specifications. For example, the Rule contains several implementation specifications that are labeled "addressable" rather than "required." (68 FR 8334, 8336 (Feb. 20, 2003).) An addressable implementation specification is not optional; rather, if an organization determines that the implementation specification is not reasonable and appropriate, the organization must document why it is not reasonable and appropriate and adopt an equivalent measure if it is reasonable and appropriate to do so. (See 68 FR 8334, 8336 (Feb. 20, 2003); 45 C.F.R. § 164.306(d) (3).)

The outcome of the risk analysis process is a critical factor in assessing whether an implementation specification or an equivalent measure is reasonable and appropriate. Organizations should use the information gleaned from their risk analysis as they, for example:

- Design appropriate personnel screening processes. (45 C.F.R. § 164.308(a) (3) (ii) (B).)

- Identify what data to backup and how. (45 C.F.R. § 164.308(a) (7) (ii) (A).) Decide whether and how to use encryption. (45 C.F.R. §§ 164.312(a) (2) (IV) and (e) (2) (ii).)

- Address what data must be authenticated in particular situations to protect data integrity. (45 C.F.R. § 164.312(c) (2).)
- Determine the appropriate manner of protecting health information transmissions. (45 C.F.R. § 164.312(e) (1).)

Important Definitions

Unlike "availability", "confidentiality" and "integrity", the following terms are not expressly defined in the Security Rule. The definitions provided in this guidance, which are consistent with common industry definitions, are provided to put the risk analysis discussion in context. These terms do not modify or update the Security Rule and should not be interpreted inconsistently with the terms used in the Security Rule.

Vulnerability: Vulnerability is defined in NIST Special Publication (SP) 800-30 as *"[a] flaw or weakness in system security procedures, design, implementation, or internal controls that could be exercised (accidentally triggered or intentionally exploited) and result in a security breach or a violation of the system's security policy."*

Vulnerabilities, whether accidentally triggered or intentionally exploited, could potentially result in a security incident, such as inappropriate access to or disclosure of e-PHI. Vulnerabilities may be grouped into two general categories, technical and non-technical. Non-technical vulnerabilities may include ineffective or non-existent policies, procedures, standards or guidelines. Technical vulnerabilities may include: holes, flaws or weaknesses in the development of information systems; or incorrectly implemented and/or configured information systems.

Threat: An adapted definition of threat, from NIST SP 800-30, is *"[t]he potential for a person or thing to exercise (accidentally trigger or intentionally exploit) a specific vulnerability."*

There are several types of threats that may occur within an information system or operating environment. Threats may be grouped into general categories such as natural, human, and environmental. Examples of common threats in each of these general categories include:

Natural threats such as floods, earthquakes, tornadoes, and landslides.

Human threats are enabled or caused by humans and may include intentional (e.g., network and computer based attacks, malicious software upload, and unauthorized access to e-PHI) or unintentional (e.g., inadvertent data entry or deletion and inaccurate data entry) actions.

Environmental threats such as power failures, pollution, chemicals, and liquid leakage.

Risk: An adapted definition of risk, from NIST SP 800-30, is:

"The net mission impact considering (1) the probability that a particular [threat] will exercise (accidentally trigger or intentionally exploit) a particular [vulnerability] and (2) the resulting impact if this should occur . . .. [R]isks arise from legal liability or mission loss due to—

- *Unauthorized (malicious or accidental) disclosure, modification, or destruction of information*
- *Unintentional errors and omissions*
- *IT disruptions due to natural or man- made disasters*
- *Failure to exercise due care and diligence in the implementation and operation of the IT system."*

Risk can be understood as a function of 1) the likelihood of a given threat triggering or exploiting a particular vulnerability, and 2) the resulting impact on the organization. This means that risk is not a single factor or event, but rather it is a combination of factors or events (threats and vulnerabilities) that, if they occur, may have an adverse impact on the organization.

Elements of a Risk Analysis

There are numerous methods of performing risk analysis and there is no single method or "best practice" that guarantees compliance with the Security Rule. Some examples of steps that might be applied in a risk analysis process are outlined in NIST SP 800-30.

The remainder of this guidance document explains several elements a risk analysis must incorporate, regardless of the method employed.

Scope of the Analysis: The scope of risk analysis that the Security Rule encompasses includes the potential risks and vulnerabilities to the confidentiality, availability and integrity of all e-PHI that an organization

43

creates, receives, maintains, or transmits. (45 C.F.R. § 164.306(a).) This includes e-PHI in all forms of electronic media, such as hard drives, floppy disks, CDs, DVDs, smart cards or other storage devices, personal digital assistants, transmission media, or portable electronic media. Electronic media includes a single workstation as well as complex networks connected between multiple locations. Thus, an organization's risk analysis should consider all its e-PHI, regardless of the particular electronic medium in which it is created, received, maintained or transmitted or the source or location of its e-PHI.

Data Collection: An organization must identify where the e-PHI is stored, received, maintained or transmitted. An organization could gather relevant data by: reviewing past and/or existing projects; performing interviews; reviewing documentation; or using other data gathering techniques. The data on e-PHI gathered using these methods must be documented. (See 45 C.F.R. §§ 164.308(a) (1) (ii) (A) and 164.316(b) (1).)

Identify and Document Potential Threats and Vulnerabilities:
Organizations must identify and document reasonably anticipated threats to e-PHI. (See 45 C.F.R. §§ 164.306(a) (2) and 164.316(b) (1) (ii).) Organizations may identify different threats that are unique to the circumstances of their environment. Organizations must also identify and document vulnerabilities which, if triggered or exploited by a threat, would create a risk of inappropriate access to or disclosure of e-PHI. (See 45 C.F.R. §§ 164.308(a) (1) (ii) (A) and 164.316(b) (1) (ii).)

Assess Current Security Measures: Organizations should assess and document the security measures an entity uses to safeguard e-PHI, whether security measures required by the Security Rule are already in place, and if current security measures are configured and used properly. (See 45 C.F.R. §§ 164.306(b) (1), 164.308(a) (1) (ii) (A), and 164.316(b) (1).)

The security measures implemented to reduce risk will vary among organizations. For example, small organizations tend to have more control within their environment. Small organizations tend to have fewer variables (i.e. fewer workforce members and information systems) to consider when making decisions regarding how to safeguard e-PHI. As a result, the appropriate security measures that reduce the likelihood of risk to the confidentiality, availability and integrity of e-PHI in a small organization may differ from those that are appropriate in large organizations.

Determine the Likelihood of Threat Occurrence: The Security Rule requires organizations to take into account the probability of potential risks to e- PHI. (See 45 C.F.R. § 164.306(b) (2) (IV).) The results of this assessment, combined with the initial list of threats, will influence the determination of which threats the Rule requires protection against because they are "reasonably anticipated."

The output of this part should be documentation of all threat and vulnerability combinations with associated likelihood estimates that may impact the confidentiality, availability and integrity of e-PHI of an organization. (See 45 C.F.R. §§ 164.306(b) (2) (IV), 164.308(a) (1) (ii) (A), and 164.316(b) (1) (ii).)

Determine the Potential Impact of Threat Occurrence: The Rule also requires consideration of the "criticality," or impact, of potential risks to confidentiality, integrity, and availability of e- PHI. (See 45 C.F.R. § 164.306(b) (2) (IV).) An organization must assess the magnitude of the potential impact resulting from a threat triggering or exploiting a specific vulnerability. An entity may use either a qualitative or quantitative method or a combination of the two methods to measure the impact on the organization.

The output of this process should be documentation of all potential impacts associated with the occurrence of threats triggering or exploiting vulnerabilities that affect the confidentiality, availability and integrity of e-PHI within an organization. (See 45 C.F.R. §§ 164.306(a) (2), 164.308(a) (1) (ii) (A), and 164.316(b) (1) (ii).)

Determine the Level of Risk: Organizations should assign risk levels for all threat and vulnerability combinations identified during the risk analysis. The level of risk could be determined, for example, by analyzing the values assigned to the likelihood of threat occurrence and resulting impact of threat occurrence. The risk level determination might be performed by assigning a risk level based on the average of the assigned likelihood and impact levels.

The output should be documentation of the assigned risk levels and a list of corrective actions to be performed to mitigate each risk level. (See 45 C.F.R. §§ 164.306(a) (2), 164.308(a) (1) (ii) (A), and 164.316(b) (1).)

Finalize Documentation: The Security Rule requires the risk analysis to be documented but does not require a specific format. The risk analysis documentation is a direct input to the risk management process.

Periodic Review and Updates to the Risk Assessment: The risk analysis process should be ongoing. In order for an entity to update and document its security measures "as needed," which the Rule requires, it should conduct continuous risk analysis to identify when updates are needed. (45 C.F.R. §§ 164.306(e) and 164.316(b) (2) (iii).) The Security Rule does not specify how frequently to perform risk analysis as part of a comprehensive risk management process. The frequency of performance will vary among covered entities. Some covered entities may perform these processes annually or as needed (e.g., bi-annual or every 3 years) depending on circumstances of their environment.

A truly integrated risk analysis and management process is performed as new technologies and business operations are planned, thus reducing the effort required to address risks identified after implementation. For example, if the covered entity has experienced a security incident, has had change in ownership, turnover in key staff or management, is planning to incorporate new technology to make operations more efficient, the potential risk should be analyzed to ensure the e-PHI is reasonably and appropriately protected. If it is determined that existing security measures are not sufficient to protect against the risks associated with the evolving threats or vulnerabilities, a changing business environment, or the introduction of new technology, then the entity must determine if additional security measures are needed. Performing the risk analysis and adjusting risk management processes to address risks in a timely manner will allow the covered entity to reduce the associated risks to reasonable and appropriate levels.

In Summary: Risk analysis is the first step in an organization's Security Rule compliance efforts. Risk analysis is an ongoing process that should provide the organization with a detailed understanding of the risks to the confidentiality, integrity, and availability of e-PHI.

There are many ways to perform risk analysis. Many practices choose to use the Security Risk Assessment Tool at https://www.healthit.gov/providers-professionals/security-risk-assessment-tool. While this tool it makes things easier for the practices to complete a risk analysis, there are many questions that need a technical background. The person who is completing the risk analysis must have sufficient technical expertise. I believe you should still use the services of someone who has technical expertise to answer the questions correctly.

There are many different other risk assessments available for download and purchase. But once again without a technical background many of the questions cannot be answered correctly. There are also tools that scan the network and based on the findings before the risk analysis. These make the technical task easier but the risk analysis also covers both the privacy and administration areas of HIPAA, so these tools must be supplemented with onsite information.

The main purpose of risk analysis, whatever tool is used, is to find possible problems and issues that may lead to data breaches or HIPAA violations. After a risk analysis is completed the next step is a risk management plan. This is where a plan is developed to address the issues that need to be fixed. The risk analysis from healthIT.Gov categorizes the risks as either required or addressable. Required are just like it states these must be addressed. The addressable are not optional but they either must be fixed or they must be explained why the practice has put an alternative safeguard of place. To stay truly HIPAA compliant, the risk analysis should be performed repeatedly, HIPAA rules state a minimum time of one year but to be truly compliant the practice should do this at least quarterly.

Chapter Ten

How do I choose a method without breaking the bank?

So, you go back online to search for the terms HIPAA compliance. You find that there are many different products that use many different systems. Many different consultants will "make you HIPAA certified." Still you don't know what it means to be HIPAA certified. So, then you go back the ONC site and read some more about HIPAA. **And the more you read the more confused you become.** You are an intelligent person because you are a dentist, but you have no idea what these rules and regulations mean. You got into dentistry to practice dentistry, not to become a lawyer or a computer tech. The biggest source of your confusion is that many of the products and consultants state that they are "HIPAA certified", but according to the ONC there is no federal certification for HIPAA. The best you can achieve is HIPAA compliant.

According to U.S. Department of Health & Human Services, there are many things that must occur both as a one-time action and on the continuing basis for a dental office to be HIPAA compliant and to stay HIPAA Compliant. There are daily, weekly, monthly, quarterly and yearly tasks that must be completed.

HIPAA is divided to three main parts:

- Technical which is your computer networks and principally deals with ePHI,
- Privacy which deals with your in-office protocols with respect to patient privacy,
- Administrative which are your office policies and procedures.

Obviously the first solution that comes to your mind is to not to worry about HIPAA. I don't think I need go into about why this will not work. This involves what we commonly refer to as the ostrich sticking your head in the sand. If you don't talk about it, it'll go away. Obviously, that's not a valid way to address this issue.

Some of the ways that I have seen practices try to achieve HIPAA compliance is to purchase a set of policies and procedures from their local foundation, or go online and find somebody else's policies and procedures and cut and paste their practice's information in place of the other practice's information in the document. They may download a check list or purchase a "HIPAA in a box software". Although it is tempting to believe that doing this will make your practice HIPAA compliant, these approaches don't even come close. A practice that is truly HIPAA compliant has policies and procedures that are tailored specifically for the individual practice, and the practice personal follow these policies and procedures. It is typically commonplace for practice to believe they are compliant because they have four-inch thick binder on the shelf gathering dust. But it has never been read or even opened. Believe it or not to be compliant you must follow the policies and procedures that are written in the manual.

Once your practice has a set of policies and procedures, your practice must also complete yearly HIPAA training. This must include everyone in your practice, from the receptionist, up to the managing dentist. This training must include not only how to follow the policies and procedures in your manual but it also talks about the penalties for violating HIPAA. And a 15-minute online course will not be enough to cover your assets if an audit occurs.

This Security Training should also include what to do if someone asks for their medical records, a notice of privacy practices, disaster recovery, and how to handle a data breach. Not only is it mandatory to have a backup plan for your practice, it is also mandatory to have a disaster recovery plan in the case of a catastrophic incident. This catastrophic incident does not have to be a tornado earthquake or hurricane, it could be a pipe bursting upstairs and flooding the server room.

Another often missed requirement is periodic security remainders. Although the number of reminders is vague you still must give your staff periodic reminders.

After reading the requirements and the ramifications of doing nothing you decide that that's just not an option for you. Even if you are never audited by the federal government or the state, a data breach or ransomware could cause your practice to go out of business. Statistically, most businesses will go out of business after the loss of their data. At the very least you'll have to pay someone some bitcoins for your data. **If you can't pay for your data, then can you reimport your entire patient data from paper. Can you really afford to do that?**

To be truly complaint, you need a solution that takes care of all three areas of HIPAA. Some practices will use three different solutions or three different people for each of the three areas of HIPAA. For example, one person for the technical, one person for the privacy and one person for the administrative areas. While this solution could work, issues will arise when there is overlap in the areas. For instance, Disaster recovery is an area that spans all three areas. Typically, when more than one person is responsible for a task does not get done.

Because Technical area is the part seems to give Practices the most issues, I have an entire section on choosing this person and method.

This Page left blank for notes.

Chapter Eleven
How do I choose a person or people to lead my Practice Compliance Program?

To begin this process, you need to decide who is going to be the expert to help with the Technical, Privacy and Administrative sections of HIPAA. Because of the seeming distant different tasks that must be completed, let's divide the process into two sections, Technical, and Privacy/ Administrative.

According to the government:

- A covered entity must designate a privacy official who is responsible for the development and implementation of the policies and procedures of the entity
- A covered entity must designate a contact person or office who is responsible for receiving complaints under this section and who is able to provide further information about matters covered by the notice required by §164.520.
- A covered entity must provide training to each member of the covered entity's workforce by no later than the compliance date for the covered entity

These regulations are more administrative then technical so that the person tasked with these must not only understand HIPAA, he must be knowledgeable about the practice policies. This person may also help to write the practice policies. This person is typically a HIPPA consultant.

The second area is technical so the practice typically assigns it to the IT guy. I want you to read on to make sure you make the right choice.

This Page left blank for notes.

Chapter Twelve
Privacy and Security Officer Job Description

Most practices designate a staff member to work with the HIPAA consultant. The HIPAA regulations state that the practice must name a Privacy and Security officer in writing.

According to the HIM Body of Knowledge™ here is a Sample (Chief) Privacy Officer Job Description:

Sample (Chief) Privacy Officer Job Description
Position Title: (Chief) Privacy Officer

Position Overview: Under HIPAA (the Health Insurance Portability and Accountability Act of 1996) every healthcare organization must designate a privacy official. The privacy official may have other titles and duties in addition to his/her privacy official designation in a typical practice or organizational setting. In terms of HIPAA compliance, the privacy official shall oversee all ongoing activities related to the development, implementation and maintenance of the practice/organization's privacy policies in accordance with applicable federal and state laws. HIPAA for purposes of this document includes HIPAA, HITECH and Omnibus requirements.

General Purpose: The Privacy Officer is responsible for the organization's Privacy Program including but not limited to daily operations of the program, development, implementation, and maintenance of policies and procedures, monitoring program compliance, investigation and tracking of incidents and breaches and insuring patients' rights in compliance with federal and state laws.

Responsibilities:
- Builds a strategic and comprehensive privacy program that defines, develops, maintains and implements policies and

processes that enable consistent, effective privacy practices which minimize risk and ensure the confidentiality of protected health information (PHI), paper and/or electronic, across all media types. Ensures privacy forms, policies, standards, and procedures are up-to-date.

- Works with organization senior management, security, and corporate compliance officer to establish governance for the privacy program.
- Serves in a leadership role for privacy compliance
- Collaborate with the information security officer to ensure alignment between security and privacy compliance programs including policies, practices, investigations, and acts as a liaison to the information systems department.
- Establishes, with the information security officer, an ongoing process to track, investigate and report inappropriate access and disclosure of protected health information. Monitor patterns of inappropriate access and/or disclosure of protected health information.
- Performs or oversees initial and periodic information privacy risk assessment/analysis, mitigation and remediation.
- Conducts related ongoing compliance monitoring activities in coordination with the organizations other compliance and operational assessment functions.
- Takes a lead role, to ensure the organization has and maintains appropriate privacy and confidentiality consents, authorization forms and information notices and materials reflecting current organization and legal practices and requirements.
- Oversees, develops and delivers initial and ongoing privacy training to the workforce.
- Participates in the development, implementation, and ongoing compliance monitoring of all business associates and business associate agreements, to ensure all privacy concerns, requirements, and responsibilities are addressed.
- Works cooperatively with the Health Information Management (HIM) Director and other applicable organization units in

overseeing patient rights to inspect, amend, and restrict access to protected health information when appropriate.

- Manages all required breach determination and notification processes under HIPAA and applicable State breach rules and requirements.
- Establishes and administers a process for investigating and acting on privacy and security complaints
- Performs required breach risk assessment, documentation, and mitigation. Works with Human Resources to ensure consistent application of sanctions for privacy violations
- Initiates, facilitates and promotes activities to foster information privacy awareness within the organization and related entities.
- Maintains current knowledge of applicable federal and state privacy laws and accreditation standards.
- Works with organization administration, legal counsel, and other related parties to represent the organization's information privacy interests with external parties (state or local government bodies) who undertake to adopt or amend privacy legislation, regulation, or standard.
- Cooperates with the U.S. Department of Health and Human Service's Office for Civil Rights, State regulators and/or other legal entities in any compliance reviews or investigations.
- Serves as information privacy resource to the organization regarding release of information and to all departments for all privacy related issues.

Qualifications:
- Baccalaureate degree in health information management or a related healthcare field.
- Knowledge and experience in state and federal information privacy laws, including but not limited to HIPAA.
- Demonstrated organization, facilitation, written and oral communication, and presentation skills.

Additional Requirements:
- Demonstrated skills in collaboration, teamwork, and problem-solving to achieve goals

- Demonstrated skills in verbal communication and listening
- Demonstrated skills in providing excellent service to customers
- Excellent writing skills
- A high level of integrity and trust
- Extensive familiarity with health care relevant legislation and standards for the protection of health information and patient privacy
- Health care legal, operational, and or financial skills.

After practices find and name their Privacy Official, they have this person develop policies and procedures. Most practices will either go online and find a procedure and policy manuals and cut and paste their information, or will take one step better and purchase a manual from their local foundation and then cut and paste. The problem with this method, although these manuals are very comprehensive, once it is edited, the practice must follow all the rules and regulations in this manual or risk breaking the law. The HIPAA manual is a dynamic manual that should be updated as conditions may change. Dentists usually will then typically assign the process to the office manager, or the dentist will handle this themselves, as if they are not busy enough.

The next position they must name is the security official. Although this area is more technical in nature there is some overlap with the Privacy official.

According to the HIM Body of Knowledge™ here is a Sample (Chief) Security Officer Job Description:

Sample (Chief) Security Officer Job Description

Position Title: (Chief) Security Officer

Position Overview: Under the HIPAA (the Health Insurance Portability and Accountability Act of 1996) Security Rule every Covered Entity (CE) and Business Associate (BA) must designate a security official. The security official may have other titles and duties in addition to his/her security official designation in a typical practice or organizational setting. In terms of HIPAA compliance, the security official shall oversee and ensure compliance with both the required and addressable, technical, administrative and physical safeguards in accordance with applicable federal and state laws, especially the HIPAA Security Rules.

General Purpose: The Security Officer is responsible for the organization's Security Program including but not limited to daily operations of the IT security program, oversight of the annual and ongoing risk assessment process, development, implementation, and maintenance of policies and procedures, ensuring the confidentiality, integrity and access of electronic protected health information and of monitoring program compliance as well as investigation and tracking of incidents and breaches and in compliance with federal and state laws.

Responsibilities:

- Builds a strategic and comprehensive information security program that defines, develops, maintains and implements policies and processes that enable consistent, effective information security practices which minimize risk and ensure the integrity, confidentiality and availability of information that is owned, controlled and processed within the organization. Ensures information security policies, standards, and procedures are up-to-date.
- Initiates, facilitates, and promotes activities to foster information security awareness within the organization.
- Creates a culture of cyber security both with the IT organization and driving behavioral changes for the business.
- Evaluates security trends, evolving threats, risks and vulnerabilities and applies tools to mitigate risk as necessary.
- Manages security incidents and events involving electronic protected health information (ePHI)

- Ensure that the disaster recovery, business continuity, risk management and access controls needs of the facility are addressed.
- Ensures the institution/organization complies with the administrative, technical and physical safeguards.
- Collaborates with organization senior management, Privacy Officer, and Corporate Compliance officer to establish governance for the security program.
- Serves in a leadership role for security compliance.
- Works closely with the Privacy Officer to ensure alignment between security and privacy compliance programs including policies, practices and investigations, and acts as a liaison to the information systems and compliance departments.
- Is responsible for initial and periodic information security risk assessment/analysis, mitigation and remediation. Responsible for development and implementation of security risk management plan.
- Ensure organization has audit controls to monitor activity on electronic systems that contain or use electronic protected health information.
- Oversee periodic monitoring and reviewing of audit records to ensure that activity is appropriate. Such activity would include, but is not limited to, logons and logoffs, file accesses, updates, edits and printing.
- Ensure the organization has and maintains appropriate system use and disclosure / confidentiality statement.
- Oversees, develops and/or delivers initial and ongoing security training to the workforce. Initiates, facilitates and promotes activities to foster information security awareness within the organization and related entities
- Participates in the development, implementation, and ongoing compliance monitoring of all BA's and business associate agreements, to ensure -security concerns, requirements, and responsibilities are addressed.

- Assists Privacy Officer as needed with breach determination and notification processes under HIPAA and applicable State breach rules and requirements.
- Establishes and administers a process for investigating and acting on security incidents which may result in a privacy breach breaches.
- Partners with Human Resources and Privacy Officer to ensure consistent sanctions for security violations
- Maintains current knowledge of applicable federal and state security laws, licensing and certification requirements and accreditation standards.
- Cooperates with the U.S. Department of Health and Human Service's Office for Civil Rights, State regulators and/or other legal entities, and organization on officers in any compliance reviews or investigations.
- Serves as information security consultant to all departments for all data security related issues.

Qualifications:
- Baccalaureate degree in information systems or a related healthcare field.
- Knowledge and experience in state and federal information security laws, including but not limited to HIPAA, including NIST, PCI and all other applicable regulations.
- Demonstrated organization, facilitation, written and oral communication, and presentation skills.
- Recommended Security certification such as Certified in Healthcare Privacy and Security (CHPS) and/or other healthcare industry related security credentials.

Additional Requirements:
- Demonstrated skills in collaboration, teamwork, and problem-solving to achieve goals.
- Demonstrated skills in verbal communication and listening.

- Demonstrated skills in providing excellent service to customers.
- Excellent writing skills.
- A high level of integrity and trust.
- Knowledge of HIPAA, state and federal guidelines on security, transactions and security.
- Extensive familiarity with health care relevant legislation and standards for the protection of health information and patient security.

The task of helping the security officer is usually given to the "Computer Guy". For most practices, this may be sufficient if this person understands HIPAA. The problem is that along with managing HIPPA and CMIA, this person must also stay current on the latest threats and changing regulations. This person must also deal with external as well as internal threats. The person must also understand how it all relates to HIPAA. Read following chapters for more information on choosing this person.

Chapter Thirteen
Managing Business Associates under the 2013 HIPAA
Omnibus Final Rule

Business Associates: In 2003 HIPAA defined health care providers and payers as Covered Entities. Organizations that support Covered Entities and encounter Protected Health Information (PHI) are Business Associates. In the past, Business Associates caused many data breaches but were out of the reach of the federal HIPAA enforcement agencies. Although they signed Business Associate Agreements stating they would protect patient data, there was no government enforcement. **The HITECH Act of 2009, a law best known for funding Electronic Health Records for doctors and hospitals, requires Business Associates to comply with HIPAA and be directly liable for HIPAA penalties. This increases the liability for Covered Entities who now will share liability with Business Associates and their subcontractors.**

HIPAA Omnibus Final Rule: In January, the US Department of Health & Human Services (HHS) released the HIPAA Omnibus Final Rule, setting specific requirements for Business Associates to comply with HIPAA. In the Final Rule were two sections that affect IT VARs/MSPs (IT Guys) and their vendors that provide data center hosting, colocation, Cloud services, and online backup. Enforcement of the Final Rule will begin September 23, 2013.

Subcontractors: The Final Rule requires Business Associates to ensure that all their downstream Subcontractors will comply with HIPAA by signing Business Associate Agreements and implementing HIPAA compliance programs, including HIPAA-specific written policies and procedures; workforce training; delivery of HIPAA-compliant services; and documenting their work with enough detail to sustain a HIPAA audit or data breach investigation. If a Business Associate shares protected data with anyone that does not comply with HIPAA, it is a data breach requiring notifying their health care client, who must then notify patients and the federal government. Penalties of up to $ 1.5 million per occurrence may apply, plus costs to notify patients, legal fees, and reputational damage control costs.

Organizations that Maintain Data: The Final Rule also requires that any person or entity that 'maintains' (stores) protected data, even if they don't look at it, is a Business Associate. Notable was that there is no exemption for encrypted data, data in locked cabinets where the owner of the facility does not have keys, or other situations where the data is not— or cannot be— accessed.

The Final Rule discusses: https://s3.amazonaws.com/public-inspection.federalregister.gov/2013-01073.pdf.

Since it could come from a Covered Entity or Business Associate, it is virtually impossible for a hosting, cloud, or backup vendor to prevent PHI from entering their system.

This article is important because it references a presentation by Leon Rodriguez, the government's chief HIPAA enforcer, who clearly says that data centers offering colocation and hosting now must comply.

http://healthworkscollective.com/onlinetech/87816/himss-13-hhs-final-ruling-changes-rules-roles-hipaa-hosting

This article from datacenterknowledge.com addresses the idea that compliance can be mixed between requirements. Note that the article was written before the Omnibus Final Rule but has some valuable information comparing various accreditations. http://www.datacenterknowledge.com/archives/2012/06/29/hipaa-compliant-data-centers/

Chapter Fourteen
Does your computer guy have to be sign a BAA?

We often read stories about the computer network that gets hacked and the practice loses all its data and the patients get their identity stolen. The problem with this is most computer consultants are good with technical issues but they typically are deficient in soft skills such as user issues and documentation. When dealing with HIPAA and computer networks, if it is not documented, it never happened.

Because we are dealing with medical and patient records, we not only have the deal with "common computer hacks" but we must deal with HIPAA and CMIA. Before not only didn't you want to deal with the federal government for a HIPAA violation; now the state and the FTC are involved.

Although Dentists have an advanced degree and are highly intelligent, the thought of dealing with computer guys makes many doctors break into a cold sweat or at least makes them feel stupid. The worst part of dealing with these computer guys is you do not know for sure what they are doing. You don't think the person is ripping you off, but how can you be sure? What about if the person charges you a lot of money, does not fix the problem and makes it worse. Now you still have the computer issue and it will cost you more money to get someone else to fix it again.

To have a computer network that is operating most efficiently and is HIPAA compliant, it must have routine maintenance performed on it. Your network is like a car, it will run okay without maintenance for a while, but after a while without any maintenance it will fail. Unless you trust your computer consultant, it is easy to be convinced he is not ripping you off but you are risking a HIPAA audit because it is often difficult to follow up on the consultant's work.

HIPAA regulations demand that this person working on your network be also HIPAA compliant. You must have a business associate agreements with them. According to DataBreaches.net **"At least 30% of breaches and 35% of breached records reported to HHS's public breach tool are attributable to third-party breaches."**

According to https://www.hhs.gov/hipaa/for-professionals/covered-entities/sample-business-associate-agreement-provisions/index.html , this is what dental Practices must have in place with any person or company that comes in contact with your practices ePHI.

Does your computer guy have to have a BAA? If you can guarantee that he will never see any PHI then he does not have to sign a BAA. I don't see how this is possible, do you. **Also, most doctors believe they are not responsible for the actions of their BAA's, but they are.**

Here is some information about this from the U.S. Department of Health & Human Services.

Is a covered entity liable for, or required to monitor, the actions of its business associates?

No. The HIPAA Privacy Rule requires covered entities to enter into written contracts or other arrangements with business associates which protect the privacy of protected health information; but covered entities are not required to monitor or oversee how their business associates carry out privacy safeguards or the extent to which the business associate abides by the privacy requirements of the contract. Nor is the covered entity responsible or liable for the actions of its business associates. **However, if a covered entity finds out about a material breach or violation of the contract by the business associate, it must take reasonable steps to cure the breach or end the violation, and, if unsuccessful, terminate the contract with the business associate.** If termination is not feasible (e.g., where there are no other viable business alternatives for the covered entity), the covered entity must report the problem to the Department of Health and Human Services Office for Civil Rights. See 45 CFR 164.504(e) (1).

With respect to business associates, a covered entity is out of compliance with the Privacy Rule if it fails to take the steps described

66

above. If a covered entity is out of compliance with the Privacy Rule because of its failure to take these steps, further disclosures of protected health information to the business associate are not permitted. In cases where a covered entity is also a business associate, the covered entity is out of compliance with the Privacy Rule if it violates the satisfactory assurances it provided as a business associate of another covered entity. https://www.hhs.gov/hipaa/for-professionals/faq/236/covered-entity-liable-for-action/index.html

Sure, sounds like you still must monitor your vendors, whether or not they are business associates.

This Page left blank for notes.

Chapter Fifteen
Sample Business Associate Contracts

A "business associate" is a person or entity, other than a member of the workforce of a covered entity, who performs functions or activities on behalf of, or provides certain services to, a covered entity that involve access by the business associate to protected health information. A "business associate" also is a subcontractor that creates, receives, maintains, or transmits protected health information on behalf of another business associate.

The HIPAA Rules generally require that covered entities and business associates enter into contracts with their business associates to ensure that the business associates will appropriately safeguard protected health information. The business associate contract also serves to clarify and limit, as appropriate, the permissible uses and disclosures of protected health information by the business associate, based on the relationship between the parties and the activities or services being performed by the business associate. A business associate may use or disclose protected health information only as permitted or required by its business associate contract or as required by law. A business associate is directly liable under the HIPAA Rules and subject to civil and, in some cases, criminal penalties for making uses and disclosures of protected health information that are not authorized by its contract or required by law. **A business associate also is directly liable and subject to civil penalties for failing to safeguard electronic protected health information in accordance with the HIPAA Security Rule.**

A written contract between a covered entity and a business associate must:
(1) Establish the permitted and required uses and disclosures of protected health information by the business associate;

(2) Provide that the business associate will not use or further disclose the information other than as permitted or required by the contract or as required by law;

(3) Require the business associate to implement appropriate safeguards to prevent unauthorized use or disclosure of the information, including implementing requirements of the HIPAA Security Rule about electronic protected health information;

(4) Require the business associate to report to the covered entity any use or disclosure of the information not provided for by its contract, including incidents that constitute breaches of unsecured protected health information;

(5) Require the business associate to disclose protected health information as specified in its contract to satisfy a covered entity's obligation with respect to individuals' requests for copies of their protected health information, as well as make available protected health information for amendments (and incorporate any amendments, if required) and accountings;

(6) To the extent the business associate is to carry out a covered entity's obligation under the Privacy Rule, require the business associate to comply with the requirements applicable to the obligation;

(7) Require the business associate to make available to HHS its internal practices, books, and records relating to the use and disclosure of protected health information received from, or created or received by the business associate on behalf of, the covered entity for purposes of HHS determining the covered entity's compliance with the HIPAA Privacy Rule;

(8) At termination of the contract, if feasible, require the business associate to return or destroy all protected health information received from, or created or received by the business associate on behalf of, the covered entity;

(9) Require the business associate to ensure that any subcontractors it may engage on its behalf that will have access to protected health information agree to the same restrictions and conditions that apply to the business associate with respect to such information; and

(10) Authorize termination of the contract by the covered entity if the business associate violates a material term of the contract. Contracts between business associates and business associates that are subcontractors are subject to these same requirements.

This Page left blank for notes.

Chapter Sixteen
What are your computer technician choices?

So, what are your computer technician choices? Can you trust a person recommended by the software vender, an independent computer consultant, or someone from your staff? Remember this person also must be your BA so he must also be HIPAA compliant.

Let's first talk about the different types of people and companies I have seen working on medical practice networks. **I want to be clear about one thing with respect to these computer types, just because your computer guy is on this list does not mean he will do a substandard job.** I just want to outline all possible risks and you should make the final decision.

The different classes of network repair solutions are listed from worst to best:

My or your cousin or brother, sister, husband, wife (you get the idea): Your brother is good with computers; as a matter of fact, he built his own computer. The computer seems to be working okay, so what if the cover has been off this computer for years. If his computer is not working then he can use his other computer or the computer at his office.

But when your receptionist's computer is not working, you don't have an endless supply of computers. After you call your brother for help, he will come over right after work because he can't get fired from his day job. So, while he finishes his work day, you wait. Maybe it is not a major issue but what if the issue is so severe, you must close for the day. By the way, is your relationship secure enough for you to fire your brother when this doesn't work out? Who will clean up a mess that was caused by an inexperienced neighbor, friend, or relative who was just trying to help? Typically fixing problems caused by inexperience computer guys is more expensive than what it would have originally cost. Their lack of experience will not allow an experienced computer technician to troubleshoot through normal processes. This will increase the final cost to fix it. The replacement techs cannot use best case examples to troubleshoot. Obviously, not all technicians are created equal. Just because a person is good with computer applications (what we call a power user) does NOT mean they know how to install and configure a firewall.

Trunk slammer: This person was recommended by one of your patients or maybe you found him in a craigslist advertisement. He is friendly and sounds knowledgeable. You think you have agree on a price before he starts working. You hire him because his rate is cheap. To keep the odds in your favor, you should only pay him after the job is completed and checked for completion. You must be aware though that sometimes a computer issue seems to be fixed but it is not. Will he return to fix the job correctly? Did he even give you an invoice that had the work he has performed outlined (mandatory HIPAA rule)? What happens if you pay him in advance? If you are paying him by the hour and he takes twice as long to finish the job, are you really saving any money? The key word here is "cheap deal". Sure, you can always find a cheaper price if you shop online or use the yellow pages, but you might end up getting the short end of the stick. As with anything in life, you get what you pay for. Companies simply cannot give you dirt cheap prices AND quality service.

If you are getting a cheap bargain, chances are you will get very little if NO service after the sale. If something goes wrong, or if you just have a question, you might find out that phone call only goes to voice mail that never gets checked, or that you must submit questions via e-mail that takes DAYS to return. How long has this person been in business and more importantly will he be in business three months from now? Can you call him back when you need service on your system? Do you really think he will honor his guarantee, if he even gave you one?

The "internal guru" at your office: Every practice, both large and small has a person that everyone in the practice goes to when they have a computer question or issue. This person can usually help them apply a Band-Aid. We refer to this person as the internal guru. This person can do the smaller jobs but for larger jobs you should probably call in someone else. Some practices feel that because "Joe the billing clerk" is pretty good at computers he could handle the security updates. All he must do is a LITTLE reading and maybe practice a little. Do you think he will research this for free? Even if you do not pay him extra money, fixing the issue will still take time away from his normal duties. Are you getting optimal use of his time? Or are you going to pay him to work on this after hours? If not, who is going to do your billing while he learns the system? Does he really know how to install, configure and troubleshoot this new device? If not, you may want to consider hiring a qualified technician to install it. Quite often, drivers and software can conflict and cause problems and unless he has installed this device before, it might be worth the small fee to get someone else to do it for you.

High school/college student: This person knows computers and has cheap rates so this is a win-win right? Typically, you find him by flyers posted at the local office supply store or from an ad on Craigslist. When you question him about whether he has even worked with your brand of software or hardware he explains that although he has not worked with your brand he has worked with a "very similar type" and they are all mostly the same. But you still may fund his education while he learns the software. In addition, are you sure he understands HIPAA and will not scare your staff and patients with his dress style and tattoos and piercings. Most people look for a part time "guru" to help them save money, but this often comes back to haunt them. If the person you have working on your machine does not do computer repair and support for a living, there is a good chance they won't have the knowledge or experience to truly help you. Technology advances at lightning speed and it takes constant learning and practice to master it. If your part-time technician is not working on PCs and dental networks every day, they probably only know enough to be dangerous.

Joe the One-Man Band: Joe may also advertise in Craigslist and may also have an ad in the yellow page. He probably has business cards and possibly signs on his car. This is the typical computer consultant. Most are hardworking and honest. When you call them, you may get voice mail or his wife, girlfriend, child etc. They take a message and you may or may not get a call back. Their rate is not overly expensive. They work from home. Typically, they do not have insurance, detailed invoices so that you are never sure what or how his work is guaranteed. If he gets hurt or breaks something will on the job, you are responsible. If he gets hurt you may have to pay his workman's comp. If he wants he can even take the practice to court to recoup damages he himself caused.

If you rely on a "one-man-band" operation, you might find yourself without any help when they go on vacation, get sick, or when they are simply too busy servicing other customers. Having multiple technicians on staff is not a guarantee of fast, reliable service, but you are far more likely to have someone to talk to when you have a problem. Another reason you want a shop that has multiple technicians is because no one computer guy – no matter how good – has infinite knowledge about every type of software, hardware, and platform. Multiple technicians mean multiple skill sets and a higher likelihood that your computer problem will get resolved faster.

What type of help desk support do they offer? If you are like me, you want to speak directly to a knowledgeable technician when you need help. However, many companies only offer e-mail and web-based support, and charge a hefty fee for anything outside of that. Do you really have time to wait or that return email that may not even help you solve the issue? Most are so overworked and overwhelmed that they can never complete the job when you need it done. Because they are stretched so tight you often cannot count on them when you really need them.

Gordon the Geek (Franchise Company): Even though they may be a big company, with thousands of technicians (geeks), they are only good as their local staff. Some of these franchises have good training programs, most don't. Most of the training that these franchises give relates to business practices such as upselling not computer technology. Even though they buy a franchise and get the logo, the franchise does not supply individual franchises with technicians. It is up to the local companies to find these workers. Chances are you may get a new unexperienced technician with an experienced tech price. If you do find a technician that you like, chances if he is any good you will not be able to get him when you need him. The word gets around quickly on which are the best techs and they are requested early and often so that you may never be able to schedule them.

Then if you have a do have problem, what type of help desk support do they offer? Will you be able to speak directly to a knowledgeable technician when you need help? However, many companies only offer e-mail and web-based support, and charge a hefty fee for anything outside of that. Which brings me to the next question…? Where is their help desk and customer service office located? Many of the big vendors are shipping their help desk support overseas to save money. While this works out great for them, it can be incredibly frustrating when you are trying to communicate with their customer support representatives. Demand that they have specific knowledge or expertise on solving your problem. Do NOT let someone practice on your machine. If they have not worked on your problem before, they should TELL you that in advance. There is too much risk involved financially and in your data and equipment.

So how do I choose? I hope the next chapter will help you.

This Page left blank for notes.

Chapter Seventeen
What is the best, most cost-effective choice?

You must hire a company that specializes in Dental Networks. When you call them with a computer problem, they should guarantee that your phone call will be either answered immediately or returned within 60 minutes or less by an experienced technician who can help. You deserve to get answers to your questions in PLAIN ENGLISH. Our technicians will not talk down to you or make you feel stupid because you don't understand their "geek speak".

Your practice should not make you to wait around all day for your computer to be repaired. We understand how important your computer is to your practice; that is why they should have offer our express service where we will start working on your computer the MINUTE you call. In most cases, they should fix it within 30 minutes or less. If you can't fix it within 30 minutes they should offer you a loaner computer so you never have your employees sitting around because the network is down.

You deserve complete satisfaction with their products and services. They should do whatever it takes to make you happy. No hassles, no problems. 100% guaranteed. A large proportion of their business should come from referrals from happy, satisfied customers. You deserve complete satisfaction with their products and services.

You should EXPECT that no damage will be done to your practice or your data. Before they start working on your computer or network, they should evaluate your problem and alert you to any potential risks involved in fulfilling your job and fill out a BAA. If there are any risks, they should be explained in full, and your authorization and agreement will be obtained before the work commences. You can also choose to have your data backed up before they start any work on your machine.

This company not only knows what a Business associate agreement is they have no problem signing it and following the terms outlined by it. They understand both computer security and HIPAA and CMIA. Business Associates are struggling to understand, implement and adapt to the regulatory standards of HIPAA. Thankfully, the changes in the law have made it mandatory for healthcare IT providers to also be HIPAA compliant. This is great news for your practice! Since your practice is now REQUIRED to use HIPAA compliant IT, it is critical that your IT provider has a deeper knowledge and understanding of HIPAA.

The proper IT provider for healthcare is known as a Managed Services Provider (MSP). HIPAA Compliant MSPs are uniquely qualified due to the way they service clients. MSPs use state-of-the-art technologies to prevent, detect, contain and correct security violations and other potential problems within your IT environment. These services are directly in line with the standards and implementations set forth by HIPAA. This according to HIPAAformsps.com.

So now that you know the different types of computer techs and companies you need to choose one.

Once you chosen a company, you also need to choose your team. This is the first step for a compliant practice. You need to decide who is going to do the actual install, configuration and office training for you on your software and HIPAA. The most important factor is the selection of privacy officer. This is by far the most important factor. You must consider if there is someone from within your organization capable and willing who can handle the task and who will take direction from your consultant.

Although most dental practices have enough work to keep a full-time Privacy officer busy all day long, most cannot afford to hire a full-time HIPAA officer. The daily little computer and HIPAA issues that come up may be just ignored. Sometimes the practice uses the staff member that may know the most about computers to fix these minor issues. This usually works well until these issues become severe enough to threaten the continued work within the practice. Then they call for a part-time computer person. But as practices migrate from paper or maybe just from Practice Management software to an integrated EDR, unexpected computer network outages are no longer just inconveniences. There is additional possibility of a HIPAA violation because of a data breech. This will lead to a corresponding loss of revenue, possible fines and embarrassment. Without initial preparation, a simple issue may explode into a major network outage and data breach that will have to be reported.

If this is the way your practice handles its computer networks and computer maintenance, your computer network person is continually putting out fires, never doing the important scheduled maintenance. (Which is mandatory according to HIPAA). Computer networks will eventually fail if scheduled maintenance is not done. Your computer network is like your car. You can go for a while without changing its oil, checking the air in the tires and so on, but eventually the car will suffer a fatal error costing much more to replace the system then it would have been to fix it. Most of the time when the network is performing okay nobody gives it a second thought. Then when it crashes everyone scrambles to find someone to fix the problem.

Think about it, is the best time to interview and find a new doctor in the emergency room when you have a life-threatening illness? You should call several techs to complete small jobs before an emergency occurs or at least interview them before depending on them to fix your network in an emergency.

You must remember there is a difference between working on a system, and also documenting it and securing it.

But what if you have a computer guy you trust? You must remember, just as there are many different types of Dentists all with different specialties, there are many different types of "computer guys". You need to choose the best option for you and your practice. Make sure your computer guy understands HIPAA. **If you choose correctly your computer network should be an investment. Your practice should be able to utilize your technology to save money and help save time.** The best way to achieve a problem free network is to make sure all maintenance is documented according to HIPAA standards.

This Page left blank for notes.

Chapter Eighteen
The Predominant IT Service Models Explained and many tricks of the trade

Okay now you have decided on a technician, how do you know that you are getting the best value for your money? Notice I didn't say the cheapest technician.

There are many tricks of the trade that so called professional companies and consultants will use to make it seem that their initial cost is lower but then they add on other costs. The final cost is much more expensive the original quote.

Comparing Apples to Apples: The Predominant IT Service Models Explained.

Before you can accurately compare the fees, services and deliverables of one IT services company to another, you need to understand the 3 predominant service models most of these companies fit within. Some companies offer a blend of all 3, while others are strict about offering only one service plan. The 3 predominant service models are:

- **Time and Materials**. In the industry, we call this "break-fix" services. Essentially you pay an agreed-upon hourly rate for a technician to "fix" your problem when something "breaks." Under this model, you might be able to negotiate a discount based on buying a block of hours. The scope of work may be simply to resolve a specific problem (like removing a virus), or it may encompass a large project like a computer network upgrade or move that has a specific result and end date clarified. Some companies will offer staff augmentation and placement under this model as well.

- **Managed IT Services.** This is a model where the IT services company takes the role of your "IT department" and not only installs and supports all the devices and PCs that connect to your server(s), but also offers phone and on-site support, antivirus, security, backup and a host of other services to monitor and maintain the health, speed, performance and security of your computer network.

- **Software Vendor-Supplied IT Services.** Many software companies will offer IT support for their customers in the form of a help desk or remote support for an additional fee. However, these are typically scaled-back services, limited to troubleshooting their specific application and NOT your entire computer network and all the applications and devices connected to it. If your problem resides outside of their specific software or the server it's hosted on, they can't help you and will often refer you to "your IT department." While it's often a good idea to buy some basic-level support package with a critical software application you use to run your business, this is not enough to provide the full IT services and support most businesses need to stay up and running.

When looking to outsource your IT support, the two service models you are most likely to end up having to choose between are the "managed IT services" and "break-fix" models. Therefore, let's dive into the pros and cons of these two options, and then the typical fee structure for both.

Managed IT Services Vs. Break-Fix: Which Is the Better, More Cost-Effective Option?

You've probably heard the famous Benjamin Franklin quote, "An ounce of prevention is worth a pound of cure." I couldn't agree more — and that's why it's my sincere belief that the managed IT approach is, by far, the most cost-effective, smartest option for any small to medium size dental practice. The only time I would recommend a "time and materials" approach is when you already have a competent IT person or team proactively managing your computer network and simply have a specific IT project to complete that your current in-house IT team doesn't have the time or expertise to implement (such as a network upgrade, installing a backup solution, etc.). Outside of that specific scenario, I do not think the break-fix approach is a good idea for General IT support for one very important, fundamental reason: you'll ultimately end up paying for a pound of "cure" for problems that could have easily been avoided with an "ounce" of prevention. If you employee a HIPAA compliant company, not only will they help with your technical areas of HIPAA, they can also help with the privacy area. This will help you stay HIPAA compliant.

In most cases, it's not cost-effective for practices with under 50 employees to hire a full-time IT person, because you can outsource this function of your business far cheaper and with a lot less work; but you DO want to hire a professional to perform basic maintenance just as you would hire an attorney to handle your legal matters or an accountant to prepare your taxes. **And if you truly understand the cost of your time and factor in employee productivity, the managed IT services model is considerably less expensive over time than the "break-fix" model.**

Why "Break-Fix" Works entirely In the Consultant's Favor, *Not* Yours

Under a "break-fix" model, there is a fundamental conflict of interests between you and your IT firm. The IT services company has no incentive to stabilize your computer network or to resolve problems quickly because they are getting paid by the hour; therefore, the risk of unforeseen circumstances, scope creep, learning curve inefficiencies and outright incompetence are all shifted to YOU, the customer. Essentially, the more problems you have, the more they profit, which is precisely what you DON'T want.

Under this model, the IT consultant can take the liberty of assigning a junior (lower-paid) technician to work on your problem who may take two to three times as long to resolve an issue that a more senior (and more expensive) technician may have resolved in a fraction of the time. There is no incentive to properly manage the time of that technician or their efficiency, and there is every reason for them to prolong the project and to find MORE problems than solutions. Of course, if they're ethical and want to keep you as a client, they *should* be doing everything possible to resolve your problems quickly and efficiently; however, that's akin to putting a German shepherd in charge of watching over the ham sandwiches. Not a good idea.

Second, it creates a management problem for you, the customer, who now must keep track of the hours they've worked to make sure you aren't getting overbilled; and since you often have no way of really knowing if they've worked the hours they say they have, it creates a situation where you really, truly need to be able to trust they are being 100% ethical and honest and tracking their hours properly (not all do). And finally, it makes budgeting for IT projects and expenses a nightmare since they may be zero dollars one month and thousands the next. Because of HIPAA regulations you must also track these repairs.

Chapter Nineteen
Why Regular Monitoring and Maintenance Is Critical for Today's Computer Networks and HIPAA

The fact of the matter is computer networks absolutely, positively need ongoing maintenance and monitoring to stay secure and HIPAA compliant. The ever-increasing dependency we have on IT systems and the data they hold — not to mention the *type* of data we're now saving digitally — have given rise to very smart and sophisticated cybercrime organizations and who work around the clock to do one thing: compromise your networks for illegal activities.

In most cases their intent is to access patient information and passwords to rob you (or your patients), create fake identities for credit card fraud, etc. In other cases, they may want to use your computer network to send illegal spam, host pirated software, spread viruses, etc. And, some do it just for the "fun" of being able to make computer systems inoperable. These criminals work around the clock in teams, constantly finding and inventing new ways to get around your antivirus software and firewalls; that's why you have to remain ever vigilant against their attacks.

Of course, this doesn't even take into consideration other common "disasters" such as rogue employees, lost devices, hardware failures (which are the #1 reason for data loss), fire and natural disasters and a host of other issues that can interrupt or outright destroy your IT infrastructure and the data it holds. Then there's regulatory compliance for any practice saving or touching credit card or financial information, medical records and even client contact information such as e-mail addresses.

Preventing these problems and keeping your systems up and running (which is what managed IT services is all about) is a LOT less expensive and damaging to your organization than waiting until one of these things happens and then paying for emergency IT services to restore your systems to working order (break-fix), not to mention the cost of re-entering lost data, if it's salvageable.

If you are not constantly monitoring your network, you run the risk of a data breach. If this occurs you will not only have to deal with angry patients you will have to deal with the state and federal government. If you do not have a Business Associate agreement with your vendors, now you have the additional risk of added violations. I cannot stress this enough, anyone that touches your network must have a BAA with your practice. These vendors must be HIPAA compliant.

Chapter Twenty
So how do they charge? Per hour, per day, per job

Hourly: Also, known as time and materials. Sounds like the best solution, you are only paying for the actual time the tech spends on sight. This sound like it will save you the most money. But you must look at the big picture; if you compare two techs each with different amounts of experience, the tech with the little experience may be using you to fund his on the training. Let's say you need him to install a firewall. He quotes a rate of $25.00 x 3 hours and the cost of the firewall, what a bargain. He tells you this job is a no brainer. But six hours later he is still trying to get the firewall to work with your EHR, he thought this firewall would work but now you must pay him to send it back and purchase a different firewall. Maybe this one will work, or maybe it won't. But you do know that your office is wide open to hackers. Also, your staff is not working because the firewall is on the network and your office staff needs the network to bill, schedule patients, send referrals and so on.

The more experienced tech will probably anticipate problems before they arise. He will be able to fix them with minimum of disruption when they do surface. You will probably end up paying more in the long run for the inexperienced tech plus the job may take longer and you may not be able to use your computer network during this time. This could not only result in not only lost billing revenues but it could also result in patients cancelling appointments. You may even lose patients who need to see a dentist but are unable to secure an appointment. So, they call another dentist. I am not saying you will not get a deal, but do you want to gamble on it. What can do if your bargain technician is still working 3 days later (8 hour x 3 days = 24 hours), and is reading the book Firewall for dummies. When he finally does finish, he bills for 4 days' pay, and he has learned a valuable skill on your dime.

Per Project: This may be the best value for the money. When a technician is experienced and has completed this task many times, he knows the fastest and the correct way to complete a task with a minimum amount of disruptions. In addition, he knows the other issues that may pop up because of changes of the interaction of different hardware and software with the installation of a new software or hardware package. If an unexpected problem occurs he will be there to fix the issue. Although the cost may seem initially to be higher in the long run the total cost comes much lower in the end, not to mention the lower stress level of the staff. Unless you have a monthly service agreement, this is usually the best way to go. You just must be sure to get a written description and guarantee before you allow the computer consultant anywhere near your network.

Monthly: Today many practices are moving to a monthly rate for all computer repairs. For this monthly rate, the practice gets a full-time computer technician at a part time rate. The practice also gets priority service when emergencies occur, but because daily, weekly and monthly routine maintenance is completed, many computer issues do not occur. This also insures that important but often overlooked tasks such as virus software update and data backups are done. These tasks must be monitored for HIPAA compliance. Although these tasks may seem trivial if not done repeatedly the consequences may be catastrophic.

Chapter Twenty-One
What is a HIPAA Compliant MSP?

A term for a company that takes care of all network support for a monthly rate is called a MSP or Managed Service Provider. According to wikipedia.org: a managed services provider (MSP) is most often an information technology (IT) services provider that manages and assumes responsibility for providing a defined set of services to its clients either proactively or as the MSP (not the client) determines that services are needed. In other words, they become one throat to choke for the practice. **Because the MSP must be a Business associate, they must be HIPAA compliant**. As part of keeping the network safe and compliant the MSP must follow HIPAA guidelines, thus ensuring the practice will be guarding against a major HIPAA violation.

If you choose a MSP company that understands HIPAA, they will be able to not only move your practice toward HIPAA compliance, they will understand the processes to make sure your practice stays there. Remember anyone you hire must be your Business Associate. You need to vet anyone that touches your ePHI, or risk audits later.

Put in the time now to hire your HIPAA compliant MSP and save yourself time and money later.

Although I know you have a million things to complete before tomorrow and I know you don't think you have room for one more thing. To have a successful project you must do some work now. Any work you do now before hiring a consultant will pay off huge dividends later.

The most important thing to remember is you and your practice deserves to have the best consultant available to complete your job. Never settle for anyone because you need someone now. The beginning of the project it is the time to find a consultant who is competent and honest. Typically, in the beginning of a project, the list of tasks needed to complete the job grows by the minute and unless you are careful some of the most important ones may get pushed back or never completed. This will come back to haunt you later. Wouldn't it be great to have a professional

91

available to not only take care of all your tasks in the beginning of a project but also anticipate all problems and issues and correct them in a timely compliant manner?

You need to know what you are looking for in a consulting company before you start to help you achieve your goals. We have all had situations where the wrong person for a job just makes things worse.

So, what are some of the common mistakes Doctors in your position have made? What were your past problems? Do you know what they were and how to stop them? Here are the most common problems Doctors make when hiring a computer consultant.

- Not giving you enough time to find the best computer consultant/ company
- Relying on chance, convenience or referral. Even a blind referral gets lucky occasionally.
- Spending too much on labor, software or hardware you don't need.
- Letting price be the most important factor
- Not being sure the consultant person is trust worthy.
- He may have fixed the big issues, but he forgot a little issue so you felt the job was not completed at all
- Let to job go way over budget, not receiving an accurate bill?
- The issue was not fixed but you didn't let him know and you felt he ripped you off.
- The consultant changed contact info and he didn't let you know.
- Or you just couldn't get him when you tried.
- Not verifying important tasks such as Backup and restores.
- Not making sure their vendors had a BAA.

If you don't take care of these issues now, it will cause you to waste money, get angry and frustrated and feel like you have been taken advantage of, not to mention the risk of a HIPAA audit or worse yet a data breach and ransomware.

Chapter Twenty-Two

Standards and implementation specifications most IT guys miss

So, you hire an IT consultant to take care of your technical area of your practice. After all an IT guy should be able handle Windows updates, patches, antivirus and so on. In addition, he should be able to install a backup solution and test this backup solution. Unfortunately, according to HIPAA, if something is not documented it is never happened. And although he has been your IT guy for a while, you are never sure what they are doing because he never tells you. You've asked for better documentation on his bills, but that just never seems to happen. Are you sure that all the mandatory maintenance is being done? And you know that it is other practices that get caught with ransomware or viruses. You just know it will never happen to you. You have antivirus on your computers and are using "HIPAA certified EHR".

I have witnessed circumstances from doctors who thought they were ok because their IT companies were around for a long time. They never verified that the work was being done. They just assumed that their data would be available when they needed it. Then after a disaster they were told that their data was not able to be restored. And before you think that the disaster will never happen to you, this disaster was a toilet overflowing and flooding the server.

As a dentist, you know that you are subject to HIPAA laws. But with the constant never-ending tasks of being a dentist and running your practice, HIPAA just seems to be pushed to the back the back of your mind. You know you must do something because it is required by both state and federal laws. You just don't know where to begin. If you don't constantly read the HIPAA laws, do you think your IT guy will? At the very least you don't even know what it means to be compliant or how to stay compliant.

Dentists and Business Associates are struggling to understand, implement and adapt to the regulatory standards of HIPAA. Anybody that encounters your ePHI even just a little bit MUST be HIPAA compliant. Since your practice is now REQUIRED to use HIPAA compliant IT, it is critical that your IT provider has a deeper knowledge and understanding of HIPAA.

The proper IT provider for healthcare is known as a Managed Services Provider (MSP). HIPAA Compliant MSPs are uniquely qualified due to the way they service clients. MSPs use state-of-the-art technologies to prevent, detect, contain and correct security violations and other potential problems within your IT environment. These services are directly in line with the standards and implementations set forth by HIPAA.

Here are the most common HIPAA standards and implementation specifications that MSPs should assist your practice with:

SECURITY MANAGEMENT PROCESS - § 164.308(a) (1)

"Implement policies and procedures to prevent, detect, contain and correct security violations."

•   Risk Analysis (Required) - § 164.308(a) (1) (ii) (A) "Conduct an accurate and thorough assessment of the potential risks and vulnerabilities to the confidentiality, integrity, and availability of electronic protected health information (ePHI)."

•   Risk Management (Required) - § 164.308(a) (1) (ii) (B) "Implement security measures sufficient to reduce risks and vulnerabilities to a reasonable and appropriate level to comply with §164.306(a)."

•   Information System Activity Review (Required) - § 164.308(a)(1)(ii)(D) "Implement procedures to regularly review records of information system activity, such as audit logs, access reports, and security incident tracking reports."

WORKFORCE SECURITY - § 164.308(a) (3)

"Implement policies and procedures to ensure that all members of its workforce have appropriate access to electronic protected health information, as provided under [the Information Access Management standard], and to prevent those workforce members who do not have access under [the Information Access Management standard] from obtaining access to electronic protected health information."

•   Authorization and/or Supervision (Addressable) - § 164.308(a) (3) (ii) (A) "Implement procedures for the authorization and/or supervision of workforce members who work with electronic protected health information or in locations where it might be accessed."

• Termination Procedures (Addressable) - § 164.308(a)(3)(ii)(C) "Implement procedures for terminating access to electronic protected health information when the employment of a workforce member ends or as required by determinations made as specified in paragraph (a)(3)(ii)(B) of this section."

INFORMATION ACCESS MANAGEMENT - § 164.308(a) (4)

"Implement policies and procedures for authorizing access to electronic protected health information that are consistent with the applicable requirements of subpart E of this part [the Privacy Rule]."

• Isolating Health Care Clearinghouse Functions (Required) - § 164.308(a)(4)(ii)(A) "If a health care clearinghouse is part of a larger organization, the clearinghouse must implement policies and procedures that protect the electronic protected health information of the clearinghouse from unauthorized access by the larger organization."

• Access Authorization (Addressable) - § 164.308(a)(4)(ii)(B) "Implement policies and procedures for granting access to electronic protected health information, for example, through access to a workstation, transaction, program, process, or other mechanism."

• Access Establishment and Modification (Addressable) - § 164.308(a)(4)(ii)(C) "Implement policies and procedures that, based upon the entity's access authorization policies, establish, document, review, and modify a user's right of access to a workstation, transaction, program, or process."

SECURITY AWARENESS AND TRAINING - § 164.308(a) (5) (I)

"Implement a security awareness and training program for all members of its workforce (including management)."

• Security Reminders (Addressable) - § 164.308(a) (S) (ii) (A) "Periodic security updates."

• Protection from Malicious Software (Addressable) - § 164.308(a) (S) (ii) (B) "Procedures for guarding against, detecting, and reporting malicious software."

- Log-in Monitoring (Addressable) - § 164.308(a) (S) (ii) (C) "Procedures for monitoring log-in attempts and reporting discrepancies."

- Password Management (Addressable) - § 164.308(a) (S) (ii) (D) "Procedures for creating, changing, and safeguarding passwords."

SECURITY INCIDENT PROCEDURES - § 164.308(a) (6)

"Implement policies and procedures to address security incidents."

- Response and Reporting (Required) - § 164.308(a) (6) (ii) "Identify and respond to suspected or known security incidents; mitigate, to the extent practicable, harmful effects of security incidents that are known to the covered entity; and document security incidents and their outcomes."

CONTINGENCY PLAN - § 164.308(a) (7) (I)

"Establish (and implement as needed) policies and procedures for responding to an emergency or other occurrence (for example, fire, vandalism, system failure, and natural disaster) that damages systems that contain electronic protected health information."

- Data Backup Plan (Required) - § 164.308(a) (7) (ii) (A) "Establish and implement procedures to create and maintain retrievable exact copies of electronic protected health information."

- Disaster Recovery Plan (Required) - § 164.308(a) (7) (ii) (B) "Establish (and implement as needed) procedures to restore any loss of data."

- Emergency Mode Operation Plan (Required) - § 164.308(a) (7) (ii) (C) "Establish (and implement as needed) procedures to enable continuation of critical business processes for protection of the security of electronic protected health information while operating in emergency mode."

- Testing and Revision Procedures (Addressable) - § 164.308(a) (7) (ii) (D) "Implement procedures for periodic testing and revision of contingency plans."

• Application and Data Criticality Analysis (Addressable) - § 164.308(a) (7) (ii) "Assess the relative criticality of specific applications and data in support of other contingency plan components."

EVALUATION - § 164.308(a) (8) (Required)

"Perform a periodic technical and nontechnical evaluation, based initially upon the standards implemented under this rule and subsequently, in response to environmental or operations changes affecting the security of electronic protected health Information that establishes the extent to which an entity's security policies and procedures meet the requirements of this subpart [the Security Rule]."

WORKSTATION USE - § 164.310(b) (Required)

"Implement policies and procedures that specify the proper functions to be performed, the manner in which those functions are to be performed, and the physical attributes of the surroundings of a specific workstation or class of workstation that can access electronic protected health information."

WORKSTATION SECURITY - § 164.310(C) (Required)

"Implement physical safeguards for all workstations that access electronic protected health information, to restrict access to authorized users."

DEVICE AND MEDIA CONTROLS § 164.310(d) (1)

"Implement policies and procedures that govern the receipt and removal of hardware and electronic media that contain electronic protected health information into and out of a facility, and the movement of these items within the facility."

• Disposal (Required) - § 164.310(d) (2) (I) "Implement policies and procedures to address the final disposition of electronic protected health information, and/or the hardware or electronic media on which it is stored."

• Media Re-Use (Required) - § 164.310(d) (2) (ii) "Implement procedures for removal of electronic protected health information from electronic media before the media are made available for re-use."

•   Accountability (Addressable) - § 164.310(d) (2) (iii) "Maintain a record of the movements of hardware and electronic media and any person responsible therefore.

•   Data Backup & Storage (Addressable) § 164.310(d) (2) (IV) "Create a retrievable, exact copy of electronic protected health information, when needed, before movement of equipment."

ACCESS CONTROL - § 164.312(a) (1)

"Implement technical policies and procedures for electronic information systems that maintain electronic protected health information to allow access only to those persons or software programs that have been granted access rights as specified in § 164.308(a)(4)) [(Information Access Management)]."

•   Unique User Identification (Required) - § 164.312(a) (2) (I) "Assign a unique name and/or number for identifying and tracking user identity."

•   Emergency Access Procedure (Required) - § 164.312(a) (2) (ii) "Establish (and implement as needed) procedures for obtaining necessary electronic protected health information during an emergency."

•   Automatic Logoff (Addressable) - § 164.312(a) (2) (iii) "Implement electronic procedures that terminate an electronic session after a predetermined time of inactivity."

•   Encryption & Decryption (Addressable) - § 164.312(a) (2) (IV) "Implement a mechanism to encrypt and decrypt electronic protected health information."

AUDIT CONTROLS - § 164.312(b) (Required)

"Implement hardware, software, and/or procedural mechanisms that record and examine activity in information systems that contain or use electronic protected health information."

INTEGRITY - § 164.312(c) (1) (Required)

"Implement policies and procedures to protect electronic protected health information from improper alteration or destruction."

PERSON OR ENTITY AUTHENTICATION (Required) - § 164.312(d)

"Implement procedures to verify that a person or entity seeking access to electronic protected health information is the one claimed."

TRANSMISSION SECURITY - § 164.312(e) (1)

"Implement technical security measures to guard against unauthorized access to electronic protected health information that is being transmitted over an electronic communications network."

- Integrity Controls (Addressable) - § 164.312(e) (2) (I) "Implement security measures to ensure that electronically transmitted electronic protected health information is not improperly modified without detection until disposed of."

- Encryption (Addressable) - § 164.312(e) (2) (ii) "Implement a mechanism to encrypt electronic protected health information whenever deemed appropriate."

NOTE - We HIGHLY recommend REQUIRING full disk encryption of EVERY mobile device and EVERY device that stores ePHI. Please remember that "Addressable" DOES NOT mean "not required".

By the way did you know that anyone who comes to contact PHI on your network must sign a business associate agreement? So, that means you are responsible for your network and you are also responsible for their network. If they do a poor job on HIPAA compliance on your network, what makes you think there can do a better job on theirs. Because they are your business associate, they are also bound by the rules and regulations of HIPAA. Unfortunately, the bad guys have discovered that if they breach just one MSP, or a computer guy's computer they will have access to many usernames and passwords of many different networks. In other words, your Computer guy's network is low hanging fruit.

Even through this person may be not been able to handle all the technical tasks of HIPAA, you are also expecting this person to handle all your administrative and privacy tasks of HIPAA. Do you see the idiocy?

And as you have seen from the text taken from HHS.gov, it is possible for an IT professional to handle some of the technical requirements but some tasks that are a hybrid between privacy and technical. For instance, when writing a disaster recovery plan, the person who is writing this plan must have firsthand knowledge of not only the technical specifications of the computer network but also must understand the business practices of the dental office.

The first and most important requirements of the practice with respect to HIPAA compliance is a risk analysis. This risk analysis must be updated yearly or when there is change within the network.

Most of the questions are technical in nature but some such as are more administrative in nature:

- Do you update your workforce members' training each time you develop and implement new policies and procedures?
- Do you document initial and continuing training?
- Do you have written job descriptions that define appropriate access to ePHI?

So, to expect your IT guy to be able to answer these questions is the same as having your teenager give herself braces after watching a YouTube video. The teenager has access to paperclips and rubber bands the same way that the IT professional has access to a boilerplate policy and procedure manual. After completion there will be something in place for both, but what will be the result?

You think your IT guy should be able handle the technical aspects of HIPAA and you think your office staff should be able to handle the administration and the privacy aspects of HIPAA. But are you sure? Are you willing risk fines, loss of patients, or embarrassment on the 6 o'clock news? How about a headline in the local newspaper saying a data breach affects your local hometown dentist (you)?

Have you ever had a patient who has done nothing to help control the health of their teeth and mouth? Not only do not get their teeth cleaned every six months. They don't floss or brush. Then they complain about having major tooth decay. Your computer network is very like this, it takes constant maintenance so that you don't have a data breach. A little bit of computer network maintenance like brushing and flossing, would go a long way to keep out and keep your networks secure but most people either don't have the time and willingness or understand why this is important. They falsely believe that because everything appears ok the network is behaving "OK".

Think of the Windows updates that are released once or twice a month as brushing your teeth. Think of the virus scans as flossing your teeth regularly to stop tooth decay. It is the same thing with respect to your computer network. It's okay for your computer guy to install antivirus and run the updates but to be truly have a compliant this must be monitored and documented. Think of the documentation as six-month cleaning, the only differences you should really look to update you documents more frequently, monthly or at the very least quarterly. Sometimes even the most conscientious person who flosses and brushes their teeth will get a cavity. That's where looking at computer logs will help to minimize any damage that may occur. Does your IT guy even know how to monitor proper access to ePHI or what to do if a data breach occurs?

Are you starting to see where it's not enough just to be an IT person? The person who controls your network should also understand HIPAA, the technical aspects of computers and a how to tailor documentation to fit your practice. This chosen person should be able to help with data breaches and to recommend to your HR department the sanctions that should be implemented.

What if your IT guy discovers a data breach? Does he know your practice process for breaches? Did he work with your HR, privacy officer and the dentist to write the practice sanction and breach policies?

I know you believe that your people are awesome and that a breach will never happen to you. The people who work for you would never sell your data. The problem is that people change and their situations change.

There was a lady who worked for health clinic who was discovered to be selling ePHI. When she was caught and questioned, she explained she had cancer and didn't have enough money to treat her cancer. You can never tell what someone will do in a desperate time.

Do you know the number one cause of computer breaches is user errors? In other words, somebody clicking on a link that they should not have or going to a website that they should not of. The best way to prevent this is by training your users. This is found in the privacy section of HIPAA, not technical section.

So, in addition to being an IT person, this person must be able to train your staff. Do you want training from someone who is condescending or somebody who will talk down to you?

Today's dental office relies more and more on their computers. Gone is the day when all a Dentist needed to run an office was just a pad of paper. In addition to having all your patient's records, scheduling and billing information on the computer, today's medical office often uses VoIP phones and online scheduling. When the computer network goes down it typically cripples the whole office. Not only does the office lose money today because they often can't see patients, they lose future revenue because they cannot bill. Many Dentists treat computer consultants the way many people treat dentists, they only call dentists when they are in pain. Dentists only call the consultant after the network crashes. This is often a recipe for failure. The person in charge of your network must become a part of your team.

To have a computer network that is operating most efficiently, it must have routine maintenance performed on it. Your network is like a car, it will run okay without maintenance for a while, but after a while without any maintenance it will fail. Unless you trust your computer consultant it is easy to be convinced he is ripping you off because it is often difficult to follow up to check on the consultant's work. Any work you do now will pay off later when you have a HIPAA compliant computer network. **After a ransomware attack is not good time to find out you have no backups.** Like everything there is a right and wrong way to do things, do you see why you should demand the person supporting your network understand HIPAA to keep your network HIPAA compliant?

I hope you can see why you need use a HIPAA compliant MSP to keep your practice safe. It is also important to perform regular maintenance on your network. This will make sure little issues today will not become major catastrophes later. **Remember when done correctly IT is an investment not an expense.**

Chapter Twenty-Three

What to Look for In A HIPAA Compliant Managed Services Agreement and What You Should Expect to Pay?

Important! Please note that the following price quotes are industry averages based on a recent IT industry survey conducted of over 750 different IT services firms. **The prices we found are NOT HIPAA complaint MSPs because we were unable to find enough to have a good cross section.** We are providing this information to give you a general idea of what most IT services firms charge and to help you understand the VAST DIFFERENCES in service contracts that you must be aware of before signing on the dotted line. We believe that it is our duty to be HIPAA compliant so that we don't charge more for this service. Please understand that this does NOT reflect our pricing model or approach, which is simply to understand exactly what you want to accomplish FIRST and then customize a solution based on your specific needs, budget and situation. These prices are NOT for a dental specific solution, and HIPAA services may also be extra. Our solutions are dental specific and HIPAA compliant for no additional cost.

Hourly Break-Fix Fees: Most IT services companies selling break-fix services charge between $90 to and $150 per hour with a two-hour minimum. In most cases, they will give you a discount of 5% to as much as 20% on their hourly rates if you purchase and pay for a block of hours in advance.

If they are quoting a **project**, the fees range widely based on the scope of work outlined. If you are hiring an IT consulting firm for a project, I would suggest you demand the following:

- **A very detailed scope of work that specifies what "success" is.** Make sure you detail what your expectations are in performance, work flow, costs, security, access, etc. The more detailed you can be, the better. Detailing your expectations up front will go a long way in avoiding miscommunications and additional fees later to give you what you REALLY wanted.

- **A fixed budget and time frame for completion.** Agreeing to this up front aligns both your agenda and the consultant's. Be very wary of loose estimates that allow the consulting firm to bill you for "unforeseen" circumstances. The bottom line is this: it is your IT consulting firm's responsibility to be able to accurately assess your situation and quote a project based on their experience. You should not have to pick up the tab for a consultant underestimating a job or for their inefficiencies. A true professional knows how to take into consideration those contingencies and plan accordingly.

Managed IT Services: Most managed IT services firms will quote you a MONTHLY fee based on the number of devices they need to maintain, back up and support. In our area, that fee is somewhere in the range of $100 to $500 per server, $35 to $125 per desktop and approximately $10 per smartphone or mobile device. If you hire an IT consultant and sign up for a managed IT services contract, here are some things that

SHOULD be included (make sure you read your contract to validate this):

- Security patches applied weekly, if not daily, for urgent and emerging threats
- Antivirus updates and monitoring
- Firewall updates and monitoring
- Backup monitoring and test restores
- Spam-filter installation and updates
- Spyware detection and removal
- Monitoring disk space on workstations and servers
- Monitoring hardware for signs of failure
- Optimizing systems for maximum speed

- Disk defrag
- Checking the surge suppressor
- Documenting all work

The following services may **NOT be included** and will often be billed separately. Make sure you review your contract carefully to know what is and are **NOT** included!

- Hardware, such as new servers, PCs, laptops, etc.
- Software licenses
- On-site support
- New computer deployment
- HIPAA compliant services
- Risk analysis

Warning! Gray areas of "all-inclusive" service contracts. To truly compare the "cost" of one managed IT services contract to another, you need to make sure you fully understand what is and isn't included and the "SLA" or "service level agreement" you are signing up for. It's very easy for one IT services provider to appear far less expensive than another until you look closely at what you are getting.

PS Any person that encounters PHI at your practice must be your Business Associate.

This Page left blank for notes.

Chapter Twenty-Four

21 revealing questions to ask your IT support firm BEFORE giving them access to your computer network, e-mail and PHI.

The following are 21 questions to ask your HIT services provider that will clarify exactly what you're getting for the money. Some of these items may not be that important to you, while others (like response time, adequate insurance and uptime guarantees) may be critical. Make sure you fully understand each of these items before deciding about who the right provider is for you; then make sure you get this IN WRITING.

Customer Service:

Q1: Do they answer their phones live or do you always have to leave a voicemail and wait for someone to call you back?

Our Answer: Our help desk answers our phones live from 7:00 a.m. to 5:30 p.m. All clients have access to our emergency after-hours number they may call if a problem arises, even on weekends. Why? Because many of the businesses we support, especially dental practices, work outside normal hours. If they cannot access their computer network and can't get hold of anyone to help them, it's not only incredibly frustrating but can be paralyzing.

Q2: Do they offer a written, guaranteed response time to your calls?

Our Answer: We guarantee to have a technician working on a problem within 60 minutes or less of your call. This is written into every service agreement we give to our clients because it's standard procedure.

Q3: Do they take the time to explain what they are doing and answer your questions in terms that you can understand (not geek-speak), or do they come across as arrogant and make you feel stupid for asking simple questions?

Our Answer: Our technicians are trained to take time to answer your questions and explain everything in simple terms. Or, as some clients prefer, our technicians simply get things up and running with virtually no involvement from them to minimize their time spent away from what matters most to them…their patients.

Q4: Do they consistently (and proactively) offer new ways to improve your network's performance, and follow new HIPAA laws or do they wait until you have a problem to make recommendations?

Our Answer: We conduct business review meetings with our clients to look for new ways to help improve their operations, lower costs, increase efficiencies and resolve any problems that may be arising. Our goal with these meetings is to help our clients be more profitable, efficient and competitive. Because we are a BA we must say HIPAA compliant so we understand how to keep your practice HIPAA compliant.

Q5: Do they provide detailed invoices that clearly explain what you are paying for?

Our Answer: We provide detailed invoices, when the work is billed, that show what work was done, why and when, so you never guess what you are paying for. We also double-check our invoices for accuracy before they are sent to you. We also   document everything done on your network, a HIPAA requirement.

Q6: Do they have adequate errors and omissions insurance, cyber as well as workers' compensation insurance to protect YOU?

Our Answer: Here's something to consider: if THEY cause a problem with your network that causes you to be down for hours or days or to lose data, who's responsible? Here's another question to consider: if one of their technicians gets hurt at your office, who's paying? In this litigious society we live in, you better make darn sure whomever you hire is adequately insured with both errors and omissions insurance AND workers' compensation — and don't be shy about asking to see their latest insurance policies!

True Story: A few years ago, Geek Squad was slapped with multimillion-dollar lawsuits from customers for bad behavior by their technicians. In some cases, their techs where accessing, copying and distributing personal information they gained access to on customers' PCs and laptops brought in for repairs. In other cases, they lost a client's laptop (and subsequently all the data on it) and tried to cover it up. Bottom line: make sure the company you are hiring has proper insurance to protect YOU.

Q7: Do they guarantee to complete projects on time and on budget?

Our Answer: All projects are fixed-priced and guaranteed to be completed on time, in writing. This is important because many unethical or incompetent computer guys will only quote "time and materials," which gives them free rein to nickel-and-dime you as well as take as much time as they want to complete a project.

Maintenance of Your Network:

Q8: Do they insist on remotely monitoring your network 24/7/365 to keep critical security settings, virus definitions and security patches up-to-date and PREVENT problems from turning into downtime, viruses, data breaches, lost data and other issues?

Our Answer: Yes; our remote network monitoring system watches over your network to constantly look for developing problems, security issues and other problems so we can address them BEFORE they turn into bigger problems. A HIPAA requirement.

Q9: Do they provide you with a weekly report that shows all the updates, security patches, and status of every machine on your network so you know for SURE your systems have been secured and updated?

Our Answer: Every week our clients get a detailed report that shows an overall health score of their network and the updates to their antivirus, security settings, patches and other important network checks (like hard-drive space, backups, speed and performance, etc.). Also, a HIPAA requirement.

Q10: Is it standard procedure for them to provide you with written network documentation detailing what software licenses you own, critical passwords, user information, hardware inventory, where ePHI is stored etc., or are they the only person with the "keys to the kingdom"?

Our Answer: All clients receive this in written and electronic form at no additional cost. We also perform a quarterly update on this material and make sure certain key people from your organization have this information and know how to use it, giving you complete control over your network. Side Note: You should NEVER allow an IT person to have that much control over you and your practice. If you get the sneaking suspicion that your current IT person is keeping this under their control as a means of job security, get rid of them (and we can help to make sure you don't suffer ANY ill effects). This is downright unethical and dangerous to your practice, so don't tolerate it! A HIPAA requirement

Q11: Do they have other technicians on staff who are familiar with your network in case your regular technician goes on vacation or gets sick?

Our Answer: Yes; and since we keep detailed network documentation (basically a blueprint of your computer network) and updates on every client's account, any of our technicians can pick up where another one has left off. All out techs are trained in the Privacy laws and background tested. A HIPAA requirement

Q12: When they offer an "all-inclusive" support plan, is it TRULY all-inclusive, or are their "gotchas" hidden in the fine print?

Our Answer: Our "all-inclusive" support plan is just that — all-inclusive. One of the more popular service plans offered by consulting firms today is an "all-inclusive" or "all-you-can-eat" managed services plan. These are actually a good thing because they'll save you a lot of money in the long run. HOWEVER, make sure you REALLY understand what is and isn't included. Some things to consider are:

- Is phone/e-mail help desk included or extra?
- What about network upgrades, moves or adding/removing users?
- Is hardware and/or software included?
- What about 3rd-party software support? (We recommend that this IS included.)
- What are the costs/consequences of early cancellation?
- What if you aren't happy with their services? Do they offer a money-back guarantee?
- If the hardware and software is included, what happens if you cancel the contract?
- Do they insist on backup/disaster recovery of your servers?
- If you have a major disaster, is restoring your network included or extra?

- What about on-site support calls? Or support to remote offices?
- Are home PCs used to access the company's network after hours included or extra?
- HIPAA compliance services

Backups and Disaster Recovery:

Q13: Do they INSIST on off-site as well as an on-site backup, or are they letting you rely on outdated tape backups or thumb drives?

Our Answer: We do not allow our clients to use thumb drive backups because thumb drive backups are incredibly unreliable. We make sure all our clients have a backup disaster recovery solution. It isn't enough to just back up your data. You need a plan that will allow you to recovery from a failure in the shortest amount of time necessary. Traditional backup methods do not! A HIPAA requirement

Q14: Do they INSIST on doing HIPAA mandatory periodic test restores of your backups to make sure the data is not corrupted and could be restored in the event of a disaster?

Our Answer: We perform a monthly "fire drill" and perform a test restore from backup for our clients to make sure their data CAN be recovered in the event of an emergency. After all, the WORST time to "test" a backup is when you desperately need it. A HIPAA requirement

Q15: Do they insist on backing up your network BEFORE performing any type of project or upgrade?

Our Answer: We do, and that's simply as a precaution in case a hardware failure or software glitch causes a major problem.

Q16: If you were to experience a major disaster, do they have a written plan for how your data could be restored FAST and/or enable you to work from a remote location?

Our Answer: All clients receive a simple disaster recovery plan for their data and network. We encourage them to do a full disaster recovery plan for their office, but at a minimum, their network will be covered should something happen. HIPPA requirement.

Technical Expertise and Support:

Q17: Is their help-desk U.S.-based?

Our Answer: We provide our own help desk and make sure the folks helping you are friendly and helpful. We consider this one of the most important aspects of customer service, plus we feel it's important to keeping your data secure.

Q18: Do their technicians maintain current vendor certifications and participate in ongoing training especially HIPAA and CMIA— or are they learning on your dime?

Our Answer: Our technicians are required to keep the most up-to-date vendor certifications and government regulations in all the software and networks we support.

Q19: Do their technicians arrive on time and dress professionally?

Our Answer: Our technicians are true professionals that you would be proud to have in your office. They dress professionally and show up on time, and if they cannot (for some odd, unforeseen reason), we always notify the client immediately. We believe these are minimum requirements for delivering a professional service.

Q20: Are they familiar with (and can they support) dental applications?

Our Answer: We own the problems with all lines of dental applications for our clients. That doesn't mean we can fix faulty software — but we WILL be the liaison between you and your vendor to resolve problems you are having and make sure these applications work smoothly for you.

Q21: When something goes wrong with your Internet service, phone systems, printers or other IT services, do they own the problem or do they say, "That's not our problem to fix"?

Our Answer: We feel WE should own the problem for our clients so they don't have to try and resolve any of these issues on their own.

Chapter Twenty-Five
What are the special software, hardware, and other things that should know and buy?

Technical Requirements You May Not Understand:

HIPAA Compliance can be a mystery. It can be even more mysterious when you don't understand technology. When you dig deep and try to understand the tasks and procedures you need to protect electronic data you are likely to encounter technical terms—and IT buzzwords— that are confusing. Here are some tips you can use to ensure that your technology foundation is secure enough to support HIPAA compliance. I have also included some equipment and software that many dentists should spend a little extra on these items, or it cost them more in the long run.

Speak Geek?

If you don't understand these terms you should contact an HIPAA Compliant IT Managed Services provider to help you evaluate your network. When it comes to surviving a HIPAA audit or data breach investigation, you need an HIPAA Compliant IT professional. Like the specialists' doctors refer patients to, and the tests that they order to see what is happening under a patient's skin, your technology must be evaluated by someone with the proper skills and experience, who must look deep into your network to identify its strengths and weaknesses. Make sure they understand the HIPAA compliance requirements you face. One way is to ask if they are a HIPAA Compliant IT Managed Services provider.

Business-class operating system:

When you turn on a computer the first thing you encounter is the operating system, usually Windows or Macintosh. What you may not know is that there are different versions, some with little or no security built in to save costs and keep prices low. Consumer versions of Windows such as Windows Home and Macintosh do not protect the files stored on the device, and do not allow you to securely connect to a network. You need to have a business-class version of the operating system and make sure it is properly set up to protect stored data and to securely join a network. This means you should not be buying computers for your network from retail stores that offer low-cost consumer products. Make sure you achieve HIPAA compliance by purchasing professional models with business-class security. The minimum Microsoft OS you should have is the pro versions.

Also, Windows XP and Microsoft Server 2003 have lost its security updates in April 2014, which means that XP computers and medical instruments with imbedded XP computers will no longer be HIPAA compliant and will be at a high risk of being breached. Office 2003 is being retired and carries the same risks. When you employ a Business-class operating system such as Windows Pro, you also have the capability to encrypt your data on the hard drive. In the case on theft this could be your "get out of jail free card".

Business-class E-mail & Text Messaging:

Webmail services like G-mail, Hotmail, Yahoo!, and those provided by your Internet Service Provider (ISP) are not secure enough to send Protected Health Information (PHI.) These services do not provide end-to-end e-mail security, and the vendors will not sign Business Associate Agreements. A small medical practice paid a $ 100,000 fine for using webmail and an online calendar for PHI. For HIPAA compliance, you need to use a secure e-mail solution provided by a secure server you own; a secure Cloud e-mail and an encryption service from a vendor that will sign a Business Associate Agreement; or by using the secure communications tools included in your certified Electronic Health Record (EHR) system. **Anytime you need to send an email it MUST be encrypted.** Faxes are OK between practices and pharmacies, unless your system converts the fax into an e-mail, which cannot be sent to a webmail account. TEXTING USING THE CELL CARRIER'S SYSTEMS IS NOT SECURE OR HIPAA-COMPLIANT. NEVER TEXT PATIENT INFO AND MAKE SURE YOUR ANSWERING SERVICE IS NOT TEXTING.

Secure Network Infrastructure:

There are two ways to set up a Windows network, a Workgroup or a Domain. A peer-to-peer Workgroup is a loosely connected group of workstations. A Domain is centrally managed and includes security features. You cannot be compliant with many HIPAA requirements like Information System Activity Review, Unique User Identification, Audit Controls, and Person or Entity Authentication in a Workgroup. You need a Domain. You may need to purchase a server, convert your existing server into a Domain Controller, or create a secure network in the Cloud. A Workgroup is a deal-breaker if you have any protected data anywhere other than your certified EHR system unless you have another way to log access and retain logs for six years. Keep that in mind all the old files you still must retain.

Encryption:

While encryption is Addressable for HIPAA compliance, if you don't have it and a device containing health information is lost or stolen, you must notify patients and report the loss to the federal government for an investigation. If a lost or stolen device is encrypted you do not have to notify patients or the government. You can purchase encryption for almost every type of computer, flash drives, CDs and DVDs. You can even purchase laptops that automatically self-encrypt when you turn them off or close the lid. In 2012 a state health department paid a $ 1.7 million penalty for a lost unencrypted hard drive. A hospital paid a $ 1.5 million fine for a lost unencrypted laptop. In 2014 a health care provider paid $ 1.725 million for losing an unencrypted laptop. Encryption costs a lot less than patient notification and fines.

Passwords and Automatic Logoff:

Yes, I know they are inconvenient and annoying. However, HIPAA compliance requires audit trails to identify which user accessed patient records. For this reason, individual users must log on and off by themselves, and not allow sharing of passwords or piggy-backing multiple users during a single session. Automatic logoff is Addressable, but the alternative choices are expensive and very inconvenient. While you do not have to use Automatic Logoff, the alternative is to NEVER (ever) allow a patient in the room with an unlocked computer. You would either have to have the doctor wait in an examining room for each patient to arrive and stay until they leave, or hire additional staff to NEVER (ever) leave a patient in a room with an unlocked computer. There are ways to make logging back on more convenient, like fingerprint readers and proximity cards. Accept the facts that you need to have each user log in and out, and that automatic logoff must be used. Like airport security and searches on the way into ball games and concerts, Security is a new way of life.

Firewall:

Your network is connected to the Internet by a router or a firewall. A router directs traffic between two networks—your internal network and the Internet. A firewall does the same, but includes security features to block unauthorized traffic to achieve HIPAA compliance. A firewall can also filter Internet traffic to prevent viruses and other malware from reaching your computers (another HIPAA compliance requirement.)

You need a business-grade firewall including the additional subscription-based features to properly protect your network. Recently a $ 400,000 fine was paid when a firewall stopped blocking unauthorized traffic and 17,500 patient records were breached. You can probably figure out that a firewall costs a lot less than the fine and the cost to notify the patients.

The Consumer versions of firewalls such as the 60-dollar consumer Firewall router bought a big box store do not have the features needed to properly secure your practice network against hacking attacks. A business class firewall with the subscription services will often stop hack attacks and ransomware before it can attack your network. This firewall will also have the capability for proactive monitoring and alerting with automated network and security reports.

A business class firewall will also allow for secure, encrypted access through the Internet for remote access remote users. For those Practices with the cloud based servers, a business class firewall will be needed to handle the increased bandwidth requirements of a cloud based server. Unlike consumer grade products, business-grade firewalls have effective intrusion prevention, anti-malware and content/URL filtering.

You also need to purchase Business class wireless access points. If you want to give your patients wireless access you need to have a WAP that has Wireless guest services to provide internet-only access for guest users. This access is separate from internal access and requires guest users to securely authenticate to a virtual access point before access is granted. You should also have a Captive portal that forces a user's device to view a page and provide authentication through a web browser before internet access is granted.

Compliant Professional IT Staff or Compliant IT Managed Services:

While it may seem like fun for a doctor to manage his/her network in his spare time, or a good role for his nephew, brother-in-law, or neighbor who can set up a home network, HIPAA compliance requires either a full-time certified staff or a Managed Services arrangement with a Complaint professional IT service provider. Complaint Managed Service Providers (MSPs) offer remote services that continually monitor and maintain your network at a fraction of the cost of a full-time IT staff.

First, networks that meet HIPAA compliance need to be configured with Security at multiple levels in mind (firewall, PC's, laptops, tablets, smart phones, and servers.) Then they must be monitored and managed to ensure that Security is still working. IT Managed Service providers use remote monitoring and management tools to continually monitor your network, identify problems before they can result in damage, and keep everything updated with security patches. When the $ 400,000 was assessed for the firewall that stopped blocking unauthorized traffic, the HIPAA enforcers noted that the problem was not detected for over 10 months and that proper system activity reviews would have alerted the medical practice much sooner. A Compliant Managed Services provider would have likely been alerted immediately. Make sure any outsourced provider signs a Business Associate Agreement and implements a HIPAA compliance program. Complaint Managed Services = HIPAA Compliance.

Chapter Twenty-Six
What does it take to get in compliance?

What does it take to move a dentist's office move with little or no HIPAA privacy safeguards in place with an unsecured computer network to a HIPAA compliant and to a secure computer network?

I will explain the actions you need to take place for this to occur. If done correctly, HIPAA compliance does not have to be a painful and expensive process. Because HIPAA was based on best network and business security practices, a good HIPAA compliance program will save the practice money. In the event of a disaster, a disaster recovery plan may keep the practice from going out of business. It will force the practices to have a good backup policy and restore policy which it may keep the practice from dealing with ransomware.

By using a systematic process, a dental practice can become HIPAA compliant and more importantly, stay HIPAA compliant. The cost to achieve this should be the about the same that they are currently paying for monthly IT support. Most practices are already doing many of the necessary tasks to stay HIPAA compliant. The most important part of a HIPAA Compliance program is documenting and keeping a record. As a computer security auditor once said, "If it wasn't documented, it never happened".

Step 1: Meet with the dentist and the practice manager to discuss the goals they need to achieve. The consultant should explain to the practice management a general overview about HIPAA, CMIA and computer security. They should have read and have become familiar with regulations. Because many of the regulations are difficult to understand, even for Lawyers, Consultants should explain regulations to the practice's staff**. (Consultants also should let them know they are not an Attorney, and cannot give legal advice.)** It is also important to set objectives about the scope of the overall compliance effort, paying careful attention to everyone's roles so that an atmosphere of compliance will be achieved.

Step 2: Decide who will be the security officer and the privacy officer. Discuss the roles of these two officers with the staff management.

Although this step seems trivial, it is extremely important. Typically, one of the first questions in an HIPAA auditor may ask is if there **documented Privacy and Security Officer**. These two people will act as liaisons between the HIPAA consultant and the practice. They also must be able to sanction employees in the event of a HIPAA, CMIA or practice violation.

Step 3: Perform a risk analysis. What a risk analysis does is that it examines and finds the areas in the practice that need to be brought up to HIPAA standards. It also documents the areas that the Practice is already compliant. There are two types of standards or safeguards: required and addressable. Required are mandatory. Addressable are also required. For addressable, the practice must decide if they want to meet the standard. If they do not want to meet the standard then the practice must explain why they choose to implement an alternative safeguard that will achieve the same result.

The risk analysis covers both privacy and security standards. To perform a proper risk analysis, the practice must employ on-site questionnaires, software tools and examine administrative documents. Sometimes there may be existing policies and procedures. If the practice already has security and privacy policies and procedures, you must take inventory of them. These may be used as is or changed to meet current standards.

The practice then must perform a Gap Analysis (determining gaps and weaknesses in office practices, policies, systems, and procedures - as they relate to HIPAA requirements between current and required practices). You must be prepared to explain why you're not following HIPAA guidelines that are "addressable," if you decide not to follow them, such as encrypting data at rest.

You must take inventory of computer/information systems (including paper records). You also need to examine all the systems to see if they store any ePHI. Then document all ePHI and PHI locations and its movement. You also must explain how you are safeguarding ePHI.

You all must see if your firewalls and operating systems are business class. Although business class firewalls cost more initially, the added security features such as audit and logging make this devices mandatory for a practice.

It is important to perform a walk through the practice to see if there any visible privacy violations such as:

- Is there PHI in the regular trash receptacle?
- Are shred containers or other PHI disposal bins available and easily accessible but secured?
- Are documents containing PHI (e.g. appointment schedules, census lists, physician orders) visible to unauthorized individuals – including the public?
- Are patient charts maintained/stored in a secure area?
- Are materials removed from printers and fax machines in a timely manner?
- Does the location have a process and designated contact for logging applicable disclosures?
- Does the location have a process for identifying and issuing patients who need to receive a Notice of Privacy Practices (NPP) and for collecting and documenting the patient's signed acknowledgement of receiving the NPP?
- Do faculty/staff log-off computers before leaving their workstations?
- Are computer monitors and printers located in secure areas, and are they positioned so that visitors can't access or view the PHI on them?
- Do staff members verify fax numbers prior to use?
- Can visitors in the waiting rooms overhear the registration process?
- Does the location have a whiteboard, patient tracker (electronic), or other posting mechanism that contains only the minimum amount of information necessary and is it located in a secure area (staff only or quasi-public area)?
- Is there PHI in the regular trash receptacle?

The Office of the National Coordinator for Health Information Technology (ONC) recognizes that conducting a risk assessment can be a challenging task. That's why ONC, in collaboration with the HHS Office for Civil Rights (OCR) and the HHS Office of the General Counsel (OGC), developed a downloadable SRA Tool [.exe - 91.3 MB] to help guide you through the process. This tool is not required by the HIPAA Security Rule, but is meant to assist providers and professionals as they perform a risk assessment.

https://www.healthit.gov/providers-professionals/security-risk-assessment-tool

The SRA Tool is a self-contained, operating system (OS) independent application that can be run on various environments including Windows OS's for desktop and laptop computers and Apple's iOS for iPad only. The iOS SRA Tool application for iPad, available at no cost, can be downloaded from Apple's App Store.

The SRA Tool takes you through each HIPAA requirement by presenting a question about your organization's activities. Your "yes" or "no" answer will show you if you need to take corrective action for that item. There is a total of 156 questions.

Resources are included with each question to help you:

- Understand the context of the question
- Consider the potential impacts to your PHI if the requirement is not met
- See the actual safeguard language of the HIPAA Security Rule
- You can document your answers, comments, and risk remediation plans directly into the SRA Tool.
- The tool serves as your local repository for the information and does not send your data anywhere else.

Completing a risk assessment requires a time investment. At any time during the risk assessment process, you can pause to view your current results. The results are available in a color-coded graphic view (Windows version only) or in printable PDF and Excel formats.

A paper-based version of the tool is also available:

- Administrative Safeguards [DOCX - 397 KB] *
- Technical Safeguards [DOCX - 312 KB] *
- Physical Safeguards [DOCX - 263 KB] *

Because some questions will require a technical background, many practices elect to use software to help complete the security portion of HIPAA. The software runs on a local computer and documents all the computer settings, logs and the like. It does not install anything on any computers. It also allows the practice to get a second opinion about their network security.

After the risk analysis is completed, you must date, print and file a hard copy of the risk analysis. Although HIPAA regulations emphasize risk analysis should be done yearly, it is best practice to complete a risk analysis at least quarterly or when any changes occur in the network.

It is also important to perform an external network vulnerability scan which will generate detailed reports showing security holes and warnings, informational items including CVSS scores, Common Vulnerability Scoring System, as scanned from outside the target network. This is important because external vulnerabilities could allow a malicious attacker access to the internal network.

Step four: After completion of the risk analysis is, the practice must create a risk management plan. A risk management plan addresses all the issues and develops mitigation actions with tasks required to minimize, avoid, or respond to risks. Beyond gathering information, a risk management plan should provide a risk scoring matrix that an organization can use to prioritize risks and appropriately allocate money and resources and ensure that issues identified are issues solved. The Risk Management plan defines the strategies and tactics the organization will use to address its risks.

Step five: After completion of the risk management plan the practice to develop or revise their existing policies and procedures. The reason that the consultant and IT guy must work with the practice, the practice must demonstrate that they are obeying and following all the policies and procedures. Within these policies and procedures are mixtures of privacy and security safeguards. Some of them include breach policies, backup and disaster recovery policies. They also include procedures to allow patients to get their data. It is important to provide a process for addressing privacy/security breaches when and if they arise. Then continually check everything to make sure you're carrying out those guidelines.

Probably the most important document that you need to have is a notice of privacy practices. This document outlines your HIPAA policy to your patients. It is the only document that most patients will see, therefore it should be done correctly. **This will act as the face of your practice.** Along with the Patient Acknowledgement of Privacy Policy, HIPAA requires healthcare providers to obtain patient acknowledgement (acceptance is not required, only acknowledgement) of the healthcare provider's privacy policy. This requirement can be met by having each patient simply acknowledge receiving a copy of the written privacy policy by signing off to that effect. If the patient refuses, a note must be made in the patient's record to indicate the refusal.

Because some patients may not be comfortable releasing private information, these documents are important to alleviate their fears. A poster with the practice's the Information Policy that explains how the practice uses patient PHI and how they properly secure this information may help to alleviate patient fears.

You must also go through and find all your business associates. By law you must document anybody who encounters your e-PHI. Also by law all your business associates must be HIPAA compliant. You must save copies of sighed BAAs.

Who is Typically a Business Associate?

Examples of service providers and vendors that are typically business associates when accessing PHI, except when acting as members of the workforce of the covered entity or of another business associate:

- Medical transcription companies
- Answering services
- Document storage or disposal (shredding) companies
- Patient safety or accreditation organizations
- Companies involved in claims processing, repricing or collections (e.g., medical billing companies)
- Health information exchanges (HIEs), e-prescribing gateways and other HIOs
- Third party administrators and pharmacy benefit managers
- Data conversion, de-identification and data analysis service providers
- Utilization review and management companies

SOMETIMES A BUSINESS ASSOCIATE

The following are examples of service providers that are sometimes business associates, depending on the underlying relationships, whether they access PHI and the functions involved:

- Accounting firms
- Auditors
- Law firms
- Consulting firms
- Software vendors and consultants
- Financial institutions (if engaging in accounts receivable or other functions extending beyond payment processing)
- ISPs, ASPs and cloud vendors
- Companies providing personal health records (business associate if providing personal health records on behalf of a covered entity)

- Researchers (if performing HIPAA functions for a covered entity)

If you are not sure you should secure a BAA, better safe than sorry.

After this a training session is required, so that everyone in the practice including the dentist and the front office staff understand the rules and regulations of HIPAA. This training should also include penalties for HIPAA breaches. Which should help to start to develop a culture of compliance in the practice. Topics that must be included are:

- Vulnerabilities that may affect ePHI
- Best ways to secure data
- Mobile Devices
- Password Maintenance
- Incident Reporting
- Viruses
- Malicious Code
- Privacy Policy

Chapter Twenty-Seven

Checklists, tasks and documentation requirements to stay in HIPAA Compliance

Because HIPAA compliance is not a one and done process, there are important tasks and procedures that must be followed daily, weekly, monthly, quarterly and yearly to remain compliant. You must have an Audit and Compliance program that is consists of ongoing monitoring and enforcement with feedback mechanism. You may have deployed new physical and technical safeguards to support your updated policies and procedures. This also includes the consistent application of sanctions for non-compliance. And don't forget to document security incident responses. Here are some of the tasks:

rver Maintenance	Minimum Frequency	Who Responsible
eate Rescue Disks	Quarterly	Automate
stall Latest Service Packs	Monthly	Automate
stall Latest OS Updates	Weekly	Automate
stall Software Updates	Weekly	Automate
stall Exchange Service Packs	Weekly	Automate
stall Exchange Updates	Weekly	Automate
eck for restores	Quarterly	IT Vendor
eck for good backups	Daily	IT Vendor
eck Event Logs	Weekly	IT Vendor
eck free space on HDDs	Daily	Automate
eck memory usage	Daily	Automate
RAID/Mirror healthy?	Daily	Automate
e UPS Batteries still good?	Daily	Automate
rify permissions on root directories	Weekly	IT Vendor
n Defrag/CheckDisk	Daily	Automate
sk Cleanup	Daily	Automate
n Scandisk	Daily	Automate
n Defrag if needed	Daily	Automate
n Prefetch	Daily	Automate
lete any program not being used	Monthly	IT Vendor
lete temp folder files, IE temp files, cookies, cache, empty recycle bin	Weekly	Automate
tivirus Software Management and Updates	Daily	Automate
ti-malware Software Management and Updates	Daily	Automate
e and Server Restores from Backup	Monthly	IT Vendor
view Logs	Daily	IT Vendor

Desktop Maintenance	Minimum Frequency	Who Resp
Install OS latest updates	Weekly	Automate
Install Software Updates	Weekly	Automate
Install latest Service Pack	Monthly	Automate
IE latest updates	Monthly	Automate
IE latest Service Pack	Monthly	Automate
Home page to company standard	Monthly	Automate
Sharing set to company standard	Monthly	IT Vendor
Disk Cleanup	Daily	Automate
Run Scandisk	Daily	Automate
Run Defrag if needed	Daily	Automate
Run Prefetch	Daily	Automate
Delete any program not being used	Monthly	IT Vendor
Delete temp folder files, IE temp files, cookies, cache, empty recycle bin	Weekly	Automate
Antivirus Software Management and Updates	Daily	Automate
Anti-malware Software Management and Updates	Daily	Automate

Security	Minimum Frequency	Who Respo
Delete unnecessary users	Monthly	IT Vendor
Check admin group for unnecessary personnel	Monthly	IT Vendor
Check other global groups and users	Monthly	IT Vendor
Strong password for Exchange Service account	Monthly	IT Vendor
Strong password for Backup service account	Monthly	IT Vendor
Strong passwords for all members of the admin group	Monthly	IT Vendor
Are password policies and restrictions used?	Monthly	IT Vendor
Check security logs	Daily	Automate
Daily firewall monitoring and updates	Daily	IT Vendor
Off-site Backup (Cloud) Storage Management	Daily	IT Vendor
Daily Monitoring of Successful Data Backup	Daily	Automate
Practice Recovery from Backup	Quarterly	IT Vendor
Firewall Management and Updates	Daily	IT Vendor
Network Resource Monitoring	Daily	IT Vendor
Automatic Problem Escalation and Resolution	Daily	IT Vendor
Content Filtering and Intrusion Protection	Monthly	Automate
Threat Testing for Employees	Quarterly	HIPAA Cons
Cybersecurity Training for Employees	Quarterly	HIPAA Cons
Penetration intrusion testing	Quarterly	IT Vendor
Review Logs	Monthly	IT Vendor
Web monitoring, social network monitoring	Daily	Automate
Spam Filtering	Daily	Automate
Risk Analysis	Yearly	HIPAA Cons
HIPAA & Security Training	Yearly	HIPAA Cons
External Penetration Test, Firewall	Yearly	IT Vendor
Internal Vulnerability Scan	Yearly	IT Vendor
EMR User Permissions and Access Audit	Quarterly	IT Vendor
Risk Management Meeting	Quarterly	IT Vendor
Security Reminders	Monthly	HIPAA Cons
EMR User Audit	Monthly	IT Vendor
Network User Audit	Monthly	IT Vendor

Documentation	Minimum Frequency	Who Responsible
IP Address Mapping	Yearly	IT Vendor
PHI flow	Yearly	IT Vendor
Print printer configurations	Yearly	IT Vendor
Print screen DHCP, WINS	Yearly	IT Vendor
Inventory printer supplies	Monthly	IT Vendor
Asset Tracking and Management	Monthly	IT Vendor
Executive Summary Monthly Report	Monthly	Automate
Vendor Liaison*	Monthly	HIPAA Consultant
Network Documentation	Monthly	Automate
Breach Notification	As Needed	HIPAA Consultant
Creation of AUP (Acceptable Use Policy)	Yearly	HIPAA Consultant
Written Disaster Recovery Plan	Yearly	IT Vendor
Documented Privacy and Security officers	Yearly	HIPAA Consultant
HIPAA/CMIA Policies tailored to you practice	Yearly	HIPAA Consultant
Updated Business Associate agreements	Yearly	HIPAA Consultant
Updated Notice of Privacy Practices (NPP)	Yearly	HIPAA Consultant
Notice of Computer security Poster	Monthly	HIPAA Consultant
Onsite Staff HIPAA Training	Yearly	HIPAA Consultant
Monthly Security Reminders	Monthly	HIPAA Consultant
Workstation, server, Fax movement log	Monthly	IT Vendor
Tracking alarm and CCTV	Monthly	IT Vendor
Documentation of Practice repairs	Monthly	HIPAA Consultant
HIPAA Risk Management Plan	Yearly	HIPAA Consultant
HIPAA Risk Analysis	Yearly	HIPAA Consultant
PHI location documentation (e.g., a PHI map)	Yearly	IT Vendor
How you've eliminated third party risks	Yearly	HIPAA Consultant
Software development lifecycles	Yearly	IT Vendor
Business associate agreements(BAA)	As Needed	HIPAA Consultant
Incident response plan/breach response plan	As Needed	HIPAA Consultant
Current/future goals and milestones	Quarterly	IT Vendor
Explanation of unimplemented addressable implementation standards	Yearly	HIPAA Consultant
Training logs	Monthly	HIPAA Consultant
Compliant processes and procedures	Yearly	HIPAA Consultant
List of authorized wireless access points	Monthly	IT Vendor
List of all devices including physical location, serial numbers, and make/model	Yearly	Automate
Lists of vendors	Monthly	IT Vendor
Lists of employees and their access to systems	Monthly	IT Vendor
Diagram of your physical office, including exit locations	Yearly	HIPAA Consultant
Disaster recovery book	Yearly	IT Vendor
Policies and procedures for the Security Rule, Privacy Rule, and Breach Notification Rule	Yearly	HIPAA Consultant

Physical Access	Minimum Frequency	Who Responsible
Is direct access to the server area restricted?	Monthly	IT Vendor
Is direct access to software restricted?	Monthly	IT Vendor
Are rescue disks secure?	Monthly	IT Vendor
Are workstations protected by password screensavers?	Monthly	IT Vendor
Physically Checking Physical Office layout	Monthly	HIPAA Consultant
Physically Cleaning of Machines	Quarterly	IT Vendor

VPN	Minimum Frequency	Who Responsible
Remote users calling the VPN have different passwords than network?	Monthly	IT Vendor
Home users with DSL or cable modems must have a personal firewall to protect their PC	Monthly	IT Vendor

IP Phone Security	Minimum Frequency	Who Responsi
Is phone system on latest revision	Monthly	IT Vendor
Is default password changed?	Monthly	IT Vendor
Check logs if abuses are taking place (give client a copy)	Monthly	IT Vendor
Is VoIP VPN access in place	Monthly	IT Vendor

Chapter Twenty-Eight

"The 10 Disaster Planning Essentials for a Dental Practice Network"

The HIPAA Contingency Plan standard requires the implementation of a disaster recovery plan. This plan must anticipate how natural disasters, security attacks, and other events could impact systems that contain PHI. These must include policies and procedures for responding to such situations. Although most dentists believe that they will never need such a plan, I have seen "minor" incidents such as a toilet overflowing or lost backup tapes cripple a practice when they were unable to restore lost data.

An HIT consultant must be able to provide their disaster recovery plan to a healthcare organization, which should include answers to questions like these:

- Where is backup data hosted? What procedure maintains retrievable copies of ePHI?
- What procedures identify suspected security incidents?
- Who must be notified in the event of a security incident? How are such incidents documented?
- What procedure documents and restores the loss of ePHI?
- What is the business continuity plan for maintaining operations during a security incident?
- How often is the disaster recovery plan tested?

If your data is important to your business and you cannot afford to have your operations halted for days – even weeks – due to data loss or corruption, then you need to read this and act on the information shared. A disaster can happen at any time on any day and is likely to occur at the most inconvenient time. If you aren't already prepared, you run the risk of having the disaster coming before you have in place a plan to handle it. This report will outline 10 things you should have in place to make sure your business could be back up and running again in the event of a disaster.

1.   Have a written plan. As simple as it may sound, just thinking through in ADVANCE what needs to happen if your server has a meltdown or a natural disaster wipes out your office, will go a long way in getting it back fast. At a minimum, the plan should contain details on what disaster could happen and a step-by-step process of what to do, who should do it and how. Also include contact information for various providers and username and password information for various key web sites. Writing this plan will also allow you to think about what you need to budget for backup, maintenance and disaster recovery. If you can't afford to have your network down for more than a few hours, then you need a plan that can get you back up and running within that time frame? **You may want the ability to virtualize your server, allowing the office to run off the virtualized server while the real server is repaired.** If you can afford to be down for a couple of days, there are cheaper solutions. Once written, print out a copy and store it in a fireproof safe, an offsite copy (at your home) and a copy with your HIT consultant.

2.   Hire a trusted professional to help you. Trying to recover your data after a disaster without professional help is business suicide; one misstep during the recovery process can result in forever losing your data or result in weeks of downtime. Make sure you work with someone who has experience in both setting up business contingency plans (so you have a good framework from which you CAN restore your network) and experience in data recovery.

3.   Have a communications plan. If something should happen where employees couldn't access your office, e-mail or use the phones, how should they communicate with you? Make sure your plan includes this information including MULTIPLE communications methods.

4.   Automate your backups. If backing up your data depends on a human being doing something, it's flawed. The #1 cause of data loss is human error (people not swapping out disks properly, someone not

setting up the backup to run properly, etc.). ALWAYS automate your backups so they run like clockwork.

5.   Have an offsite backup of your data. Always, always, always maintain a recent copy of your data off site, on a different server, or on a storage device. Onsite backups are good, but they won't help you if they get stolen, flooded, burned or hacked along with your server.

6.   Have remote access and management of your network. Not only will this allow you and your staff to keep working if you can't go into your office, but you'll love the convenience it offers. Plus, your HIT staff or an IT consultant should be able to access your network remotely in the event of an emergency or for routine maintenance. Make sure they can.

7.   Image your server. Having a copy of your data offsite is good, but keep in mind that all that information must be RESTORED someplace to be of any use. If you don't have all the software disks and licenses, it could take days to reinstate your applications (like Microsoft Office, you EHR, your database, accounting software, etc.) even though your data may be readily available. Imaging your server is like making an exact replica; that replica can then be directly copied to another server saving an enormous amount of time and money in getting your network back. Best of all, you don't have to worry about losing your preferences, configurations or favorites. To find out more about this type of backup, ask your HIT professional.

8.   Network documentation. Network documentation is simply a blueprint of the software, data, systems and hardware you have in your company's network. Your IT consultant should put this together for you. This will make the job of restoring your network faster, easier AND cheaper. It also speeds up the process of everyday repairs on your network since the technicians don't have to spend time figuring out where things are located and how they are configured. And finally, should

disaster strike, you have documentation for insurance claims of exactly what you lost. Again, have your HIT professional document this and keep a printed copy with your disaster recovery plan.

9.   Maintain Your System. One of the most important ways to avoid disaster is by maintaining the security of your network. While fires, floods, theft and natural disasters are certainly a threat, you are much more likely to experience downtime and data loss due to a virus, worm or hacker attack. That's why it's critical to keep your network patched, secure and up-to-date. Additionally, monitor hardware for deterioration and software for corruption. This is another overlooked threat that can wipe you out. Make sure you replace or repair aging software or hardware to avoid this problem.

10.   Test, test, test! A study conducted in October 2007 by Forrester Research and the Disaster Recovery Journal found that 50 percent of companies test their disaster recovery plan just once a year, while 14 percent never test. If you are going to go through the trouble of setting up a plan, then at least hire an IT pro to run a test once a month to make sure your backups are working and your system is secure. After all, the worst time to test your parachute is AFTER you've jumped out of the plane.

Chapter Twenty-Nine
Disaster Recovery Audit Checklist

Are you at risk?

There are 3 steps to this process:

1. Identify all data and IT-related functions (like credit card processing, documents on your file server, member web portal, a CRM system, critical applications, ePHI etc.) you have in place.
2. Classify the **importance** of the data and functions you've identified.
3. Apply an appropriate backup and disaster recovery plan to match the value and importance of each asset.

Use the following rating system on the impact to your business if you suffered a significant outage or complete loss of the data and processes you've identified:

0% = Zero Impact

20% = Annoying but Recoverable

40% = Minor Damage with Loss

60% = Disaster with Considerable Loss

80% = Major Disaster with Significant Loss

100% = Total Loss

When assessing costs, be sure to factor in loss of tangible sales, client goodwill, costs for re-keying (typing) the data (or any other recovery costs) as well as legal costs associated with failure to deliver on contractual obligations, potential lawsuits, etc.

Data or Business Function	If you lost access to this data/functionality **for a week or more**, what impact would it have on your business?	If you lost this data/functionality **permanently**, what impact would it have on your business?	**Estimated Cost** (Include cost of recreating data, entering it, loss of business, etc.)
Accounting Information			
Client Data (CRM)			
E-mail			
Contracts and Legal Documents			
Custom Software and Code			
Web sites and content			
Video and Audio recordings			
Patient Data			
Dental Equipment Configuration			
Total Costs:			

How often do you perform a full back up?		
Every hour	- 200	
Every day	- 100	
Weekly	+ 100	
Monthly	+ 200	
Do you keep paper records (or scans) you could reference as a source for re-entering lost a?		
Yes	- 100	
No	+ 100	
Who has access to your computer network? eck all that apply)		
Trusted, computer-savvy employees	- 100	
Trusted IT support company	- 50	
Unskilled workers/transitional staff	+ 100	
Cleaning crew, maintenance	+ 200	
Where is your data stored?		
Don't know	- 200	
On tape drives, USB devices	- 100	
Onsite hard drive	- 50	
Offsite in the cloud	+ 100	
Do you live in an area or office building that has experienced any of these disasters OR that a high potential for one of these disasters to occur? eck all that apply)		
Tornado, hurricane or severe storm	+ 100	
Earthquake	+ 100	
Terrorist attack	+ 100	
Fire/problem with another tenant	+ 100	
Flood	+ 100	
Do you store sensitive data that must be protected by law? (Medical records, credit cards, ial security numbers, financial data, etc.)		
No	- 100	
Yes	+ 200	
Do you routinely download and backup all data stored on 3rd party cloud applications (web files for example)?		
Yes	- 200	

No	+ 200	
How old is your server and/or other workstations that contain <u>critical data</u>?		
Under a year old	- 100	
1-3 years old	+ 50	
3-4 years old	+ 200	
Over 4 years old	+ 300	
Regarding disaster recovery and business continuity, check all that apply:		
You DO have a written disaster recovery plan	- 200	
You review & update your plan regularly	- 100	
You conduct periodic tests of your plan	- 100	
You DO have an inventory of assets for insurance	- 100	
How often do you perform a full back up?		
Every hour	- 200	
Every day	- 100	
Weekly	+ 100	
Monthly	+ 200	
Do you keep paper records (or scans) you could reference as a source for re-entering lost data?		
Yes	- 100	
No	+ 100	
Who has access to your computer network? (Check all that apply)		
Trusted, computer-savvy employees	- 100	
Trusted IT support company	- 50	
Unskilled workers/transitional staff	+ 100	
Cleaning crew, maintenance	+ 200	
Where is your data stored?		
Don't know	- 200	
On tape drives, USB devices	- 100	
Onsite hard drive	- 50	
Offsite in the cloud	+ 100	

Do you live in an area or office building that has experienced any of these disasters OR that [?] a high potential for one of these disasters to occur? [?]eck all that apply)		
Tornado, hurricane or severe storm	+ 100	
Earthquake	+ 100	
Terrorist attack	+ 100	
Fire/problem with another tenant	+ 100	
Flood	+ 100	
Do you store sensitive data that must be protected by law? (Medical records, credit cards, [?]ial security numbers, financial data, etc.)		
No	- 100	
Yes	+ 200	
Do you routinely download and backup all data stored on 3rd party cloud applications (web [?] files for example)?		
Yes	- 200	
No	+ 200	
How old is your server and/or other workstations that contain critical data?		
Under a year old	- 100	
1-3 years old	+ 50	
3-4 years old	+ 200	
Over 4 years old	+ 300	
Regarding disaster recovery and business continuity, check all that apply:		
You DO have a written disaster recovery plan	- 200	
You review & update your plan regularly	- 100	
You conduct periodic tests of your plan	- 100	
You DO have an inventory of assets for insurance	- 100	

Scoring: 0 or Less: Low to No Risk

You either don't have very much critical data on your computer or your backup plan is well designed. If this exercise revealed one or two areas you are NOT securing well, you now can resolve those areas immediately.

0-200: Medium Risk

Depending on what data is compromised, you will most likely be able to recover it without major catastrophic costs or consequences. HOWEVER, there are certain areas that are more important than others. For example, if you had sensitive data lost or stolen, the consequences from that could be extensive in the form of legal fees, lost customers, lost market share, a harmed reputation and possibly even a lawsuit.

200 Or More: High Risk

Your Practice is extremely vulnerable to various data-erasing disasters, and there is a high chance that you would NOT be able to recover it at all. It is imperative that you strengthen your current backup, security and disaster recovery plan immediately.

"93% of companies that lost their data for 10 days or more filed for bankruptcy within one year of the disaster, and 50% filed for bankruptcy immediately."

(Source: National Archives and Records Administration in Washington)

Chapter Thirty

Interview and Document Request for HIPAA Security Onsite Investigations and Compliance Reviews by DHH

DEPARTMENT OF HEALTH & HUMAN SERVICES

Office of E-Health Standards and Services

Sample - Interview and Document Request for HIPAA Security Onsite Investigations and Compliance Reviews

1. Personnel that may be interviewed
   - President, CEO or Director
   - HIPAA Compliance Officer
   - Lead Systems Manager or Director
   - Systems Security Officer
   - Lead Network Engineer and/or individuals responsible for:
     - administration of systems which store, transmit, or access Electronic Protected Health Information (EPHI)
     - administration systems networks (wired and wireless)
     - monitoring of systems which store, transmit, or access EPHI
     - monitoring systems networks (if different from above)
   - Computer Hardware Specialist
   - Disaster Recovery Specialist or person in charge of data backup
   - Facility Access Control Coordinator (physical security)
   - Human Resources Representative
   - Director of Training
   - Incident Response Team Leader
   - Others as identified....

2. Documents and other information that may be requested for investigations/reviews
   a. Policies and Procedures and other Evidence that Address the Following:
      - Prevention, detection, containment, and correction of security violations
      - Employee background checks and confidentiality agreements
      - Establishing user access for new and existing employees
      - List of authentication methods used to identify users authorized to access EPHI
      - List of individuals and contractors with access to EPHI to include copies pertinent business associate agreements
      - List of software used to manage and control access to the Internet
      - Detecting, reporting, and responding to security incidents (if not in the security plan)
      - Physical security
      - Encryption and decryption of EPHI
      - Mechanisms to ensure integrity of data during transmission - including portable media transmission (i.e. laptops, cell phones, blackberries, thumb drives)
      - Monitoring systems use - authorized and unauthorized
      - Use of wireless networks
      - Granting, approving, and monitoring systems access (for example, by level, role, and job function)
      - Sanctions for workforce members in violation of policies and procedures governing EPHI access or use
      - Termination of systems access

1

- Session termination policies and procedures for inactive computer systems
- Policies and procedures for emergency access to electronic information systems
- Password management policies and procedures
- Secure workstation use (documentation of specific guidelines for each class of workstation (i.e., on site, laptop, and home system usage)
- Disposal of media and devices containing EPHI

b. Other Documents:
  - Entity-wide Security Plan
  - Risk Analysis (most recent)
  - Risk Management Plan (addressing risks identified in the Risk Analysis)
  - Security violation monitoring reports
  - Vulnerability scanning plans
    o Results from most recent vulnerability scan
  - Network penetration testing policy and procedure
    o Results from most recent network penetration test
  - List of all user accounts with access to systems which store, transmit, or access EPHI (for active and terminated employees)
  - Configuration standards to include patch management for systems which store, transmit, or access EPHI (including workstations)
  - Encryption or equivalent measures implemented on systems that store, transmit, or access EPHI
  - Organization chart to include staff members responsible for general HIPAA compliance to include the protection of EPHI
  - Examples of training courses or communications delivered to staff members to ensure awareness and understanding of EPHI policies and procedures (security awareness training)
  - Policies and procedures governing the use of virus protection software
  - Data backup procedures
  - Disaster recovery plan
  - Disaster recovery test plans and results
  - Analysis of information systems, applications, and data groups according to their criticality and sensitivity
  - Inventory of all information systems to include network diagrams listing hardware and software used to store, transmit or maintain EPHI
  - List of all Primary Domain Controllers (PDC) and servers
  - Inventory log recording the owner and movement media and devices that contain EPHI

Chapter Thirty-One
Checklist: Responding to an OCR Investigation or Audit

The Office of Civil Rights (OCR), which is responsible for enforcing provisions of the Health Insurance Portability and Accountability Act (HIPAA), has contracted with a consultant to conduct 150 audits of hospitals and other covered entities by the end of 2012. The following checklist may help healthcare organizations prepare for these audits.

Policies and Standards

- ☐ Are there written policies and standards addressing the matter raised in the complaint or audit request?

- ☐ Are the relevant policies and standards consistent with the HIPAA regulations in all respects?

- ☐ Are the policies and standards generally consistent with the information security safeguards recommended by the National Institute for Standards and Technology (NIST), OCR Guidance, and other recognized authorities, commensurate with the size, complexity, and financial resources of the entity?

Training and Awareness

- ☐ Are workforce members made aware of the policies and standards relevant to the matter raised in the complaint? How?

- ☐ Is the training and education on the policies and standards documented?

- ☐ Is it timely?

Corrective Action and Discipline

- ☐ If an impermissible use or disclosure occurred through employee misconduct; were the responsible individual(s) disciplined?

- ☐ Was the disciplinary action documented?

- ☐ Was the discipline taken proportional to the actual or potential harm caused?

- ☐ Was the discipline taken consistent with the applicable policies and standards?

- ☐ Was another appropriate corrective action taken to prevent a future occurrence? Is it documented?

- ☐ Was the corrective action timely and reasonably effective?

Other Mitigation

- ☐ Did the organization take other steps to mitigate against potential harm to the individuals(s) (e.g., preventing further use or disclosure, or protection from identity theft fraud)?

- ☐ Did the organization issue an apology to the affected individual(s)?

Safeguards

- ☐ Have safeguards been implemented to reasonably protect against the type of impermissible use or disclosure presented in the complaint?

- ☐ In the case of an audit, have the safeguards recommended by the appropriate authorities, such as NIST, been implemented?

- ☐ Have all significant gaps identified in the risk assessment been addressed in the risk management plan for the entity? If not, can you demonstrate alternative safeguards or reasonable efforts to address the gaps?

- ☐ Has particular attention been paid to the safeguard lapses found in previous OCR and OIG HIPAA audits of covered entities—e.g., wireless transmission security, workforce termination procedures, identity and access management, vulnerability and patch management, contingency planning, security incident procedures, event logging, and auditing?

Source: This checklist was shared by George Rousis, director, corporate compliance and audit services, Halifax Health, Daytona Beach, Fla. (george.rousis@halifax.org).

A document obtained by *Computerworld* from a reliable source indicates that a covered entity was presented with a list of 42 items that HHS officials wanted information on within 10 days. Specifically, the CE was asked to provide policies and procedures for:

1. Establishing and terminating users' access to systems housing electronic patient health information (ePHI).
2. Emergency access to electronic information systems.
3. Inactive computer sessions (periods of inactivity).
4. Recording and examining activity in information systems that contain or use ePHI.
5. Risk assessments and analyses of relevant information systems that house or process ePHI data.
6. Employee violations (sanctions).
7. Electronically transmitting ePHI.
8. Preventing, detecting, containing and correcting security violations (incident reports).
9. Regularly reviewing records of information system activity, such as audit logs, access reports and security incident tracking reports.
10. Creating, documenting and reviewing exception reports or logs. Please provide a list of examples of security violation logging and monitoring.
11. Monitoring systems and the network, including a listing of all network perimeter devices, i.e. firewalls and routers.
12. Physical access to electronic information systems and the facility in which they are housed.
13. Establishing security access controls; (what types of security access controls are currently implemented or installed in hospitals' databases that house ePHI data?).
14. Remote access activity i.e. network infrastructure, platform, access servers, authentication, and encryption software.
15. Internet usage.
16. Wireless security (transmission and usage).
17. Firewalls, routers and switches.
18. Maintenance and repairs of hardware, walls, doors, and locks in sensitive areas.
19. Terminating an electronic session and encrypting and decrypting ePHI.
20. Transmitting ePHI.
21. Password and server configurations.

22. Antivirus software.
23. Network remote access.
24. Computers patch management.
25. Please provide a list of all information systems that house ePHI data, as well as network diagrams, including all hardware and software that are used to collect, store, process or transmit ePHI.
26. Please provide a list of terminated employees.
27. Please provide a list of all new hires.
28. Please provide a list of encryption mechanisms use for ePHI.
29. Please provide a list of authentication methods used to identify users authorized to access ePHI.
30. Please provide a list of outsourced individuals and contractors with access to ePHI data, if applicable. Please include a copy of the contract for these individuals.
31. Please provide a list of transmission methods used to transmit ePHI over an electronic communications network.
32. Please provide organizational charts that include names and titles for the management information system and information system security departments.
33. Please provide entity wide security program plans (e.g System Security Plan).
34. Please provide a list of all users with access to ePHI data. Please identify each user's access rights and privileges.
35. Please provide a list of systems administrators, backup operators and users.
36. Please include a list of antivirus servers, installed, including their versions.
37. Please provide a list of software used to manage and control access to the Internet.
38. Please provide the antivirus software used for desktop and other devices, including their versions.
39. Please provide a list of users with remote access capabilities.
40. Please provide a list of database security requirements and settings.
41. Please provide a list of all Primary Domain Controllers (PDC) and servers (including UNIX, Apple, Linux and Windows). Please identify whether these servers are used for processing, maintaining, updating, and sorting ePHI.
42. Please provide a list of authentication approaches used to verify a person has been authorized for specific access privileges to information and information systems.

Chapter Thirty-Two

Our San Diego HIT Compliance Program

Our compliance program provides what it takes to help your Practice become HIPAA/CMIA complaint and stay in compliance. We include both Privacy and Security rules.

The HIPAA Privacy Rule deals with Protected Health Information (PHI). The HIPAA Security Rule (SR) deals with electronic Protected Health Information and is divided into 3 parts. The HIPAA Security Rule requires implementation of three types of safeguards: 1) administrative, 2) physical, and 3) technical. We help you with these.

Our simple 5-step process helps to take the complex government regulations and work with your practice to meet to changing HIPAA rules.

Step 1 – We help you to choose a Privacy and Security Officer.

Step 2 – We perform an onsite Risk Assessment of your practice. Develop an action plan to see what needs to be done. We use a combination of automated tools and onsite interviews.

The Risk Assessment must include:

1) Physical Safeguards
2) Administrative Safeguards
3) Technical Safeguards
4) Policies and Procedures
5) Organizational Requirements (breach notification) (BAA)

After Risk Assessment, we will then create the Risk Management Plan:

We will Identify the Threats and Vulnerabilities, by who, what, when needs to be done

Step 3 – We tailor Privacy and Security Policies and Procedures to your practice and other documents. We will also keep track of:

- Completed checklists
- Security Risk Analysis report(s)
- Risk management action plan
- Business associate (BA) agreements
- Trainings for staff
- System monitoring results
- Policies and procedures
- Meeting minutes

Step 4 – We develop Business Associate Agreements for all your venders. We make sure all your vendors have BAA's.

Step 5 – We come Onsite and have Training for your Employees at your practice

When we are finished, your practice will have:

- Documented Privacy and Security officers with updated job descriptions for them
- HIPAA/CMIA Policies tailored to you practice
- HIPAA/CMIA Procedures designed with your practice in mind.
- Updated Business Associate agreements for all your vendors.
- Trained staff with updated documentation.
- Updated Notice of Privacy Practices (NPP)
- Notice of Computer security practices to Post in your office
- Risk Assessment of your practice and an action plan to keep your practice compliant.

Go to sandiegohit.com for more info.

I have GREAT news. In fact, this could be the single most valuable thing I could give you, and I'm doing it for free. Here's the scoop...

Because HIPAA and IT security is such an IMPORTANT topic, I've put together a series of weekly HIPAA/ IT security tips to show you and your employees how to drastically reduce your chances of being a victim of cybercrime.

Since we already do this for our clients, it doesn't cost me anything to include you as well. Plus, I want to do everything I can to educate Practice owners and their employees about how to avoid being low-hanging fruit for cybercrime. I've seen the devastation firsthand and, believe me, you do NOT want to fall victim.

Seriously, these weekly e-mails – and the strategies they contain – could save you from getting your bank account wiped out, getting your clients' personal information stolen, losing critical data and having your systems down for extended periods of time, not to mention the bad PR, civil and criminal lawsuits and fines that can result from a data breach. They also help meet the requirement for periodic security reminders.

Every week we'll focus on a single, simple thing you can do to avoid a data breach. These e-mails will come from John@sandiegohit.com and will have "IT Security Tip #X" in the subject line. Go to dandiegohit,com/HIPAA

I'll also alert you IMMEDIATELY if I see any new threats developing that you need to be on high alert for. Those e-mails will have the subject line "Urgent Security Alert: New Threat Detected" so you know to read those right away and remind all your employees to be on the lookout for that particular threat. They will detail what the threat is, and our recommendation on what you need to do to protect your practice.

If you have any questions, email me at john@janazz.com or john@sandiegohit.com or call or text me at 619-600-6865

John A Zanazzi

P.S. – If you want a more thorough approach to educating your employees about security best practices, I can also put together an HIPAA policy for your practice and train your employees on how to avoid data breaches and

cyber-attacks.

This Page left blank for notes.

www.ingramcontent.com/pod-product-compliance
Lightning Source LLC
Chambersburg PA
CBHW021950170526
45157CB00003B/928